PAULINE CAIRNS SPEITEL began her career in Scots dictionaries with the Scottish National Dictionary, continuing in 2002 with the formation of Scottish Language Dictionaries. Pauline has worked on many projects with SLD including the 2005 Supplement to the Scottish National Dictionary and was a major contributor to the latest publication of the second edition of the Concise Scots Dictionary.

FIONA ALCORN joined Scottish Language Dictionaries in 2017, having formerly lectured in the linguistic history of Scots at the University of Edinburgh.

ANN FERGUSON joined the SLD team of Editors in 2010. From a career in financial services, Ann segued to the world of Scots lexicography via a degree in English Language and Linguistics from the University of Edinburgh.

CHRISTINE ROBINSON served as SLD's Director from 2004 until her retirement in 2015. She has taught Scots to hundreds of students at a number of Scottish Universities and is (co-)author of multiple Scots language titles, including *Scotspeak: A Guide to the Pronunciation of Modern Urban Scots* and *Modren Scots Grammar*.

MAGGIE SCOTT is the founding contributor of SLD's Scots Word of the Week. She ran the column from its inception in 2005 until 2008, when she moved to the University of Salford, where she is now a Senior Lecturer in English Literature and Language and Associate Director of English and Creative Writing. Maggie has also taught Scots and English language and linguistics at the Universities of Glasgow and Edinburgh and what is now the Royal Conservatoire of Scotland.

D1188966

100
FAVOURITE
SCOTS
WORDS

Edited by
PAULINE CAIRNS SPEITEL

Luath Press Limited
EDINBURGH
www.luath.co.uk

First published 2019

ISBN: 978–1–912147–99–1

The paper used in this book is recyclable. It is made from low chlorine pulps produced in a low energy, low emission manner from renewable forests.

Printed and bound by iPrint Global, Ely

Typeset in 10.5 point Sabon by Lapiz

Contents

Foreword

Introduction

1. AFFRONT
2. AHINT
3. ANNAKER'S MIDDEN
4. AVIZANDUM
5. BAFFIES
6. BAM
7. BARRY
8. BEEK
9. BEJANT
10. BLACKMAIL
11. BLELLUM
12. BOORACH
13. BUCKIE
14. CADGER
15. CAIRD
16. CAPERCAILZIE
17. CARLIN, CARLINE
18. CARNAPTIOUS, CURNAPTIOUS
19. CHORE, CHORIE
20. CLABBYDHU
21. COLLIE BUCKIE
22. CONVOY
23. DAIDLE
24. DEVAL
25. DICHT
26. DINGIE, DINGY
27. DISJASKIT
28. DIZZY

29. DOUP, DOWP
30. DUX
31. DWAM
32. ELDRITCH
33. ETTLE
34. FANKLE
35. FERNTICKLE
36. FIRST FIT
37. FLEG
38. FURRY BOOTS CITY
39. GADGIE
40. GLAIKIT
41. GOWAN
42. HAFFET
43. HAGGIS
44. HANTLE
45. HAUGH
46. HOGMANAY
47. JALOUSE
48. JOCK
49. LALDIE. GIE SOMETHING LALDIE
50. LET-DE-CAMP
51. LORNE SAUSAGE
52. LUNCART
53. MAR
54. MINCE
55. NUMPTY
56. ONDING
57. PAGGER
58. PARTAN
59. PAWKIE
60. PECH

61. PIECE
62. PLAID, PLAIDIE
63. PURVEY
64. SCAFFIE
65. SCALDIE
66. SCART
67. SCOMFISH
68. SCOOBY
69. SCUNNER
70. SCUTTER
71. SHAN
72. SHILPIT
73. SHUNKIE, SHUNKEY
74. SKELF
75. SKITE
76. SLAISTER
77. SMIT
78. SNED
79. SNOTTUM
80. SOOK
81. SOUTER
82. SPEEL
83. SPIRTLE
84. STAIRHEID RAMMY
85. STOOKIE
86. STRAMASH
87. STRAVAIG
88. STUSHIE
89. SUMPH
90. SWALLIE
91. SYBOE
92. TENT

93. THRAPPLE

94. TUMSHIE

95. VAUNTIE

96. WEAN

97. WERSH

98. WIDDERSHINS

99. YEUKIE

100. YULE

Foreword

EDITORS AT SCOTTISH Language Dictionaries have supplied *The Herald* newspaper with a steady stream of Scots Words of the Week since 2005. By my reckoning, that's more than 700 words to date. Each article in this long-running series is a 350-word nugget of painstaking scholarship that brings to light – and sometimes to life – the breadth and depth of the meanings and usages of a single piece of Scots vocabulary.

The present anthology includes a selection of 95 contributions from four of our former and current editors plus five previously unpublished pieces. The selection of 95 was made by Pauline Cairns Speitel, our Senior Editor, who truly agonised over what to include, or rather what to leave out. To this core selection, Pauline has added articles for *bam*, *dux*, *mar*, *shunkie*, and *stravaig*, which she has penned especially for this 'wee book', as she lovingly refers to it. Together, these 100 words provide a tiny glimpse into the richness and resilience of Scots vocabulary and the preoccupations of those who use it.

In declaring 2019 the Year of Indigenous Languages, the United Nations intends to raise awareness 'not only to benefit the people who speak these languages, but also for others to appreciate the important contribution they make to our world's rich cultural diversity.' This perfectly describes our aspirations for this wee book too.

Rhona Alcorn
CEO, **Scottish Language Dictionaries**

Introduction

MORE THAN A decade ago, Scottish Language Dictionaries contacted *The Herald* about starting a Scots Word of the Week column. The intention then and now is to bring the riches of the *Dictionary of the Scots Language* (DSL) (www.dsl.ac.uk) to a wider audience.

These articles were distilled from the mighty DSL which is in fact two dictionaries: *A Dictionary of the Older Scottish Tongue* (DOST), which covers the earliest records through to 1700 in 12 volumes and which was 70 years in the making (1931 to 2002); and *The Scottish National Dictionary* (SND) which documents the vocabulary of Scots from 1700 to 1976 in ten volumes and which took a mere 45 years to compile (1931 to 1976).

In 2001, the bodies responsible for these dictionaries combined to form a new organisation, Scottish Language Dictionaries Ltd (SLD). SLD's first goal was to digitise DOST and SND and to combine them to form the online DSL. Its second mission was to add a supplement to SND.

The digitisation of DOST and SND was undertaken by the University of Dundee's English Language Department under the leadership of the late Victor Skretkowicz. The resulting DSL was made freely available online in 2004. During the digitisation phase, Iseabail Macleod and I compiled a supplement to SND, which updated the DSL to 2005.

After the publication of the 2005 SND supplement, Maggie Scott, one of our former editors, approached *The Herald* with her proposal for a column focusing on a single Scots word each week. *The Herald* was quick to see the potential and so began what has become a long-standing series. When Maggie left SLD in 2008, the baton was picked up by SLD's then director, Chris Robinson, who ran the column almost single-handedly until her retirement in 2015. Authorship then passed to me and (occasionally) my fellow editor, Ann Ferguson. Latterly, Jeremy Smith, former Convener of SLD's Board of Trustees and Professor of English Philology at the University of Glasgow, has led from the helm.

Although initially daunted by the responsibility of taking over this task, I have always approached it with enthusiasm. It has its challenges too, of course: the discipline of keeping to just 350 words greatly concentrates the mind, and one has to be ever mindful that *The Herald* is a family newspaper, which rules out a wheen of words from the DSL.

I was thrilled when this book was first suggested by Luath Press and delighted to be asked to select 100 words from the column's back catalogue, although I knew I had a hard chore ahead of me. Where to start? With more than ten years of columns to choose from, the selection process was not easy. The diversity of coverage – from obsolete Older Scots words to the language spoken by today's Scots – made the task, shall we say, tricky. And as a native of Edinburgh and a specialist in Modern Scots, I had to guard against skewing my selections to present-day Edinburgh or Central Belt Scots.

I have tried instead to choose words that represent the diversity of Scots across time and space and that show that it can veer from very formal legal language, for example Chris' article on *avizandum* (consideration of a case out of court), to the language of the playground, as shown in my article on *collie buckie* (a piggy back). Ann Ferguson's piece on *luncart* (a temporary shelter) is one of a number of studies which add a time depth to this anthology.

To ease their transition from newspaper to book, I have lightly edited some of the original articles. I hope not to have diminished the author's original voice in the process. All of the articles include a number of authentic examples drawn from the DSL's vast collection of quotations, which richly illustrate a centuries-long tradition of writing in Scots. I appreciate that the language of the examples might prove challenging for some: in those cases, I have added a gloss (for individual words) or footnote (for longer stretches) to help elucidate the excerpt.

Luath suggested I also include some words that had not yet been published in *The Herald*: these are included here for the first time. They were chosen for all the reasons listed above but of course they come with only my voice and therefore are mostly modern Scots.

I hope that in reading this book, readers will gain an insight into the scope of Scots as a living, breathing entity with a great heritage and continuum in both past and present times. I also hope that it will go some way into dispelling the myths that sometimes surround Scots either as a dead language, ie one that no one now speaks or understands, or even worse as 'slang'. Please enjoy.

Pauline Cairns Speitel

AFFRONT *verb* to cause to feel ashamed

This comes from French *afronter*, meaning to strike on the forehead and, hence, to insult. The French word in turn goes back to *frons*, the Latin for forehead. Affront is not uncommon in English but Scots, seemingly in habitual paroxysms of black burning shame, have a particular partiality for the past participle. During my teenage years, my mother was regularly black affrontit at the shortness of my skirts. The DSL reveals some other causes and consequences of embarrassment. The theatre is none too respectable in Fergus Mackenzie's *Cruisie Sketches* (1893): 'I'm sair affrontit that she should set the countryside speakin' in that play-actin' business.'

Table etiquette causes discomfiture in Susan Ferrier's *Marriage* (1818): 'Div ye mind hoo ye was affronted because I set ye doon to a cauld pigeon-pie, an' a tanker o' tippenny... afore some leddies?' SR Crockett in *The Raiders* (1894) draws attention to sartorial impropriety: 'At your time o' life, Jen, to dress up for a young man, I'm black affrontit.' In R Trotter's *Galloway Gossip* (1901) it is clear that a refusal of hospitality might cause offence: 'Mr O – wusna the man tae affront folk by refusin their offers o' refreshment.' There are various metaphors for hiding one's shame but this from George Macdonald's *Sir Gibbie* (1879) suggests extreme mortification: 'I... wuss him sae affrontit wi' himsel' er' a' be dune, 'at he wad fain hide his heid in a midden.'

Overexposure brings immunity in JB Salmond's *My Man Sandy* (1899): 'What needs I care whuther fowk kens a' aboot it, or no'? I've been black affrontit that often, I dinna care a doaken noo what happens.' However, an insult, even in jest, can have regrettable consequences as this proverb from A Henderson's collection warns: 'Affront your friend in daffin, and tine him in earnest.'[1]

Chris Robinson

---

[1] *Affront your friend in jest and lose him in earnest.*

AHINT *adverb, adjective, preposition* behind

As an adverb, ahint can refer to place or time. This example in the DSL from Robert Ford's *Tayside Songs* (1895) makes light of misfortune: 'When Fortune jooks ahint An' scuds ye wi' her broom.' In Sir Walter Scott's *The Bride of Lammermuir*, ahint means 'later in time': 'Mysie, kill the brood-hen without thinking twice on it; let them care that come ahint'

As an adjective, we find it in the sense of 'behind' schedule in Isabella Darling's *Poems* (1889): 'There was a time I channert sair like you, Oor wark ahin' and weans aye in my road.' The clock's ahint means it is slow.

The DSL often classes as adverbs words which modern grammarians might be more inclined to view as adjectives. This is particularly the case where the verb 'to be' is involved as in WA Scott's article on the 'The Vernacular of Mid-Nithsdale', in the *Transactions of the Dumfries and Galloway Antiquarian Society* (1925): 'Hurry up, we're gaun tae be clean ahint.' If we think what other words we might put here, we see that ahint is really not an adverb. We might say 'We're gaun tae be slow', but we could not say 'We're gaun tae be slowly.'

When it comes to recognising parts of speech, we are on safer ground with prepositions, but even here some of the senses may be unfamiliar. The usual sense is 'behind', as in 'ahint the dyke' but, in the north-east, it can also mean 'after', as in 'ahint thon cairry-on last week, ye wadna ken whit tae expect'. It is in the north-east, too, that we find rare examples of ahint used as a conjunction. This startling one comes from Donald Campbell's *Kirsty's Surprise* (1930): 'I've gotten snippets o' 't, but, ahin auld Leebie yokit tae gie me the news, she crackit the plate o' her fause teeth on a pan-drop I gied her.'

Chris Robinson

ANNAKER'S MIDDEN *noun* a mess, a shambles

The DSL's earliest example of the above phrase used in this sense from Central Scotland in 1962. This was firstly interpreted in the dictionary as 'a knacker's midden.' Later research, recorded in the 2005 supplement, suggested that it originated instead from: 'Annacker's, a Glasgow pork butcher from 1853 to 1942; their messy bins were frequently raked through by the poor.'

Michael Munro in his *Patter, Another Blast* from 1988 traces the origin to a firm of pork butchers, sausage makers and ham curers: 'Founded in 1853, at its height it was a chain of sixteen branches all over the city. The company also owned a sausage factory the last location of which was Naipiershall Street (near St George's Cross). The People's Palace has in its collection the shop sign from the Bridgeton Cross Branch.'

A quotation from Edinburgh in 1959 shows that as it spread eastwards, the phrase had developed an extended meaning: 'There's the Knacker's midden at it again. Said of a person who is voracious.'

However, the original meaning of a scene of general chaos is still very much with us, as illustrated by an example from a guide to Scottish speech in the *Daily Mail* of 16 September 2005: 'ANNACKER'S MIDDEN: A mess, a dreadful muddle.' Greg Hemphill and Ford Kiernan writing in *Still Game* from 2004 describe a house after a 'flitting' as: 'Look at this. It's like Annicker's Midden.'

Pauline Cairns Speitel

AVIZANDUM *noun* the consideration of a case out of court

Green's Encyclopaedia of the Laws of Scotland (1909) states avizandum is 'the term employed when the Court takes further time for the consideration of a cause, instead of pronouncing an immediate decision upon it. The Court is said to "take the case ad avizandum" or to "make avizandum of the case".' This Latinate word is one of the many Scottish legal terms that is not heard in English Courts. We find it in documents from the early 17th century. *The Diary of Sir Archibald Johnston of Wariston* (1639) records that, *The King went to a privat avisandum.*

More recently, *The Hawick Express* (22 August 1924) reports: 'Sheriff Orr said that he would take this motion to avizandum, and adjourned the diet until Thursday of next week.' It starts to appear in a literary context with Allan Ramsay (1721): 'Since dously ye do nought at Random, Then take my Bill to Avisandum' and, in William Alexander's *Johnny Gibb of Gushetneuk* (1871) we read: 'Sandy Peterkin took the subject of the two marriages to avizandum.'

The word has even crossed the Atlantic to appear in *Avizandum* by Robert Henderson, an abstract of which appears in the New Yorker (1967): 'The children speak as if he came from another world' (he emmigrated from Scotland when he was 17). He recalls how his father often took things 'ad avizandum, an old Scottish law term meaning "under advisement or scrutiny".' This is very much how my own mother used it, especially when she wished to prevaricate.

A particularly couthie example comes from a dialogue about a game of draughts in J Mackinnon's *Braefoot Sketches* (1897): 'Fat pleases me wi' the souter's play, lads, is the wy 'at he shifts withoot ever thinkin' aboot it. He's byous knackie at the shifts. Jeames, again, he tak's a' his tae avisnawdum [avizandum].'

Chris Robinson

BAFFIES *noun* slippers

These comfortable items have been gaining linguistic ground over the course of the last century. *The Transactions of the Scottish Dialects Committee* (1914) give three references to 'baffs' which they define as 'Old loose slippers, Coarse slippers used by women in the house and Large loose slippers', used also to describe animals' feet: 'What baffs o' paws the cat has.'

The DSL has nothing further to say on the matter apart from a brief addition in the first supplement recording the use of the diminutive 'baffie' in Angus and Fife in 1975 and of the participial adjective 'baffied' in the sense of wearing baffies, from *The Sunday Post* (1956).

When we get to the *New Supplement* online, however, there is no shortage of colourful quotations. In *The Scotsman* (1991), we read: 'Quick as a flash she slips on her baffies, skites up the close stairs to her neighbour's and chaps at the door.' The *Daily Record* (1997) speculates on 'a shoe-in for the Tories and Norma Major's baffies might yet be under the Number 10 table.' David Kay's show at the Edinburgh Festival in 2003 is described in *Scotland on Sunday* as 'more like a one-bar electric fire gently warming a pensioner's baffies than a comedy inferno.'

Terpsichoreal feats are described in the *Daily Mail* (2003): 'There were moments when they made the Red Arrows display team look like a squad of clumsy oafs, as students traced perfect figures of eight around and between each other, their feet flying across the floor like Darcey Bussell in feather baffies.' More prosaic is this offering from the *Sunday Mail* (2004): 'Shuffle into the kitchen in my baffies this morning to discover Sammy [the dog] has six eggs, two of Louis' school socks and a wooden spoon in her basket.'

Chris Robinson

BAM *noun* a stupid or incredulous person

Scots is a language rich in insulting vocabulary. When bam was first added to the 2005 supplement to the DSL it was thought to be a reduced form of bampot, which in its turn, is thought to be a Scots version of English *barmpot* – 'a pot for storing barm; also *figurative*, an eccentric or mad person.' (*Oxford English Dictionary* [OED] definition)

When revising the *Concise Scots Dictionary*, the editors discovered another and more likely etymology. The word is indeed probably a reduced form, but from bamboozle. In the OED, to bam someone meant to trick or deceive a person and was noted in 1738 by Jonathan Swift: 'Her Ladyship was plaguily bam'd.' A story intended to impose upon the credulous was noted earlier in *The Life & Character of Harvey the Conjuror* (1728) 'He called the Profession of a Doctorship, in Physic, a Bamm upon the world...'

However, when it came to be used to describe a credulous or stupid person in Scots is unknown; our earliest example comes from William McIlvanney's *The Big Man* published in 1985: 'Two canny play patience ya bam.' It is still used, in the 21st century, to question the intellectual capacity of some people as in this example, describing the behaviour of *Outlander* fans when visiting ancient sites in Scotland, demonstrates: 'Nothing biles my bleed mair than desecration of ancient sites. This is Clava Cairns. Johnny Foreigner – you're perfectly welcome to come ower and hae a wee shooftie. You're NAE welcome to grafitti the place and knock chunks oot o' it! Get oot o' my country ya bams (fuming).' (From the *Mail Online*, 23 August 2017)

Pauline Cairns Speitel

BARRY *adjective* something very good of its type

The DSL defines the above as 'fine; smart used to describe something very good of its type.' The first recorded mention in the DSL is from the *Roxburghshire Word-book* – 'A barrie gadjee'[1] (1923) – and it states that it's borrowed from the Gypsy dialect of Kirk Yetholm.

That this is originally a gypsy word is in no doubt, but wider research has ante-dated this in Scotland to the late 19th century. Walter Simson, who published his father's collected work on Scotland's gypsies' language found it to be attested by 12 of his informants (*A History of the Gipsies, with Specimens of the Gipsy Language*, 1865. Facsimile by Elibron Classics, 2007).

In the early 20th century, Andrew McCormick in his *Tinkler-Gipsies of Galloway* even conversed with gypsies in their own language: 'As I passed I said, "Barrie davies, nawken" (Good day, Tinkler)', although he does not record the 'Tinkler's' response.

Quite when this passed into general Scots speech is unclear. The earliest example of use by a non-gypsy is from Duncan Maclean in his short story 'Pig Squealing' published in *New Writing Scotland 10* (1992): 'Well, you wouldn't've been taking the morning off college to look after your wee baby sister and we wouldn't've met ever. And we wouldn't be sitting here now getting on barrie.'

The ultimate etymology is unclear, but Heinrich Moritz Gottlieb Grellmann, writing in his *Dissertation on the Gipsies* records a similar word, 'Baro', meaning 'great' (1787) and suggests a 'Hindostan' root.

Pauline Cairns Speitel

---

[1] Gadjee *(also spelt* gadgie*) a man*

BEEK *verb* to warm; *noun* the act of basking in the sun, a glimmer of light

The origin of this verb is unclear but to quote the *Oxford English Dictionary*, 'Now only Scots and northern dialect' and in their suggested etymology they explain that there could be a Germanic connection: 'compare, in same sense, dialect German, *bächeln, bächern...*'

The first occurrence in Scots comes from John Barbour's epic *The Bruce* and appears in the DSL: 'Ane Ynglis man, that lay bekand Hym by a fyre'[1] (1375).

The word seems to have been constant in Scots throughout the centuries and one of the earliest examples in Modern Scots comes from the poet Allan Ramsay writing in a poem of 1723: 'Her Cheek, where Roses free from Stain, in Glows of Youdith beek'.[2] Later examples include the more straightforward 'Ah'll go an' beek mysel' in the sun.' (Argyllshire, 1929). An extended meaning 'to add fuel to fire' appears in *The Gallovidian* in 1910: 'Wee Cupid beeks the fire.' However, the original meaning was still current in the late 20th century: '...but then, the sun jist cam beelin in the windaes, beekin us.' (JE McInnes writing in *A Tongue in Yer Heid*, 1994)

It also survives strongly in the Scottish Travellers community: '... and you could walk in the black dark and not even see a beak of a light...' (recorded in *A Traveller in Two Worlds. Volume One: The Early Life of Scotland's Wandering Bard*, David Campbell and Duncan Williamson in conversation, published 2011).

Pauline Cairns Speitel

---

[1] *An English man, that lay warmed him by a fire*
[2] *Youdith: youth*

BEJANT *noun* a first-year student

A bejant is a first-year student at a Scottish university, now most commonly St Andrews. The origin of the word is interesting; it is derived from the French *bejaune* which in turn is a contraction of *bec jaune* meaning yellow beak, a young bird, hence a novice or inexperienced person.

Bejant, which has been in use at least since the 18th century, has appeared in various forms including bejan, bajan, baijen, bejaunt, bejaune and bigent, some of which support its French origins. Among the examples in the DSL are this from *Alec Forbes of Howglen* by George MacDonald (1865): 'Ye'll easy fa' in wi' some lang-leggit bejan that'll be prood to instruc' ye', and this from William Tennant's *Anster Fair* (1871): 'Up from their mouldy books and tasks had sprung Bigent and Magistrand to try the game.'

Bejant has in turn spawned a few derivatives of its own, as illustrated by the quote from JH Burton's *The Scot Abroad* (1864): 'The statute of the Universitas states that a variety of predatory personages fall on the newly-arrived bejaune, demanding a bejaunica, or gratuity.' And a female first-year student may be referred to as a bejantine or bejantina, as in this not entirely serious reference from *To a Bejantina in College Echoes* (1912): 'She swam into my ken – the line's by Keats – A bejantina with her hair in pleats!'

Finally, there is the baijen hole, which is explained in the following extract from Robert Chambers' *Traditions of Edinburgh* (1825): 'A shop which all old Edinburgh people speak of with extreme regard and affection – the Baijen Hole – situated... opposite to the Old Tolbooth. The name... seems to bear reference to the Baijens or Baijen Class, a term bestowed in former days upon the junior students in the college.'

Ann Ferguson

BLACKMAIL *noun* payment extorted by intimidation

The origin of the term blackmail is Scots and the DSL informs us that blackmail is now used in Standard English 'to mean any kind of payment extorted by intimidation or pressure.'

The term is made up from black plus Scots mail or meal which meant 'rent, payment in money or kind made under lease.' Black-mail or black-meal, as it was originally coined, basically meant protection money. In 1771, T Pennant in *A Tour in Scotland* observed: 'A contribution called the black meal, was raised by several of these plundering chieftains, over a vast extent of country: whoever payed it had their cattle ensured, but those who dared to refuse were sure to suffer.'

Although this was thought by some to be mostly a Borders activity engaged upon by the notorious Borders Reivers, the *Statistical Account of Scotland* records the following information from Perthshire: 'Obliging the inhabitants to pay them, Black Meal, as it is called, to save their property from being plundered.'

When law and order eventually put an end to the Scots' habit of plundering and reiving, the term was still remembered historically as in this example from *The Aberdeen Free Press* of 9 October 1886: 'However, it would have been very easy when leading the horse up a stiff, lonely brae for a band of ruffians to have jumped from behind some bank and demanded black-mail.'

And finally, an example from a scholarly paper quoted in the *Falkirk Herald* of 6 February 1954: 'In a paper entitled, *Blackmail in Stirlingshire* Mr Mackenzie said that blackmail was a 17th century practice. The word 'blackmail' was originally a Scottish term. It was derived from the Gaelic word *mail* meaning rent or subsidy, and in the 17th century, blackmail meant the payment of money or other gratuity to thieves for their protection.'

Pauline Cairns Speitel

BLELLUM *noun* an idle, ignorant, talkative man

Blellum is one of my personal favourite Scots words and I wish it would come back into popular use. That it is still used or known at all is largely due to Robert Burns' epic poem *Tam o' Shanter* penned in 1790 where Tam is described as a 'blethering, blustering, drunken blellum'. In so few words, we have a picture of a talkative, sometimes boastful, possibly diminutive, man. Blellums to my mind are always male.

Its use in Scots is not confined simply to Burns. The DSL reveals that the word also appears in John MacTaggart's *Gallovidian Encyclopedia* of 1824 where he defines it as 'an ignorant talkative fellow.' From Lanark in 1895, William Stewart in his *Lilts and Larks frae Larkie* describes a character in the terms: 'Thus he raved, the senseless blellum.'

Although many recent usages do indeed refer to Tam, there are some instances which do not. Pete Fortune writing in the anthology *A Tongue in Yer Heid* (1994) describes a character thus: 'In face auld Tosh (bad auld blellum he is, mind ye)…' This seems to me to call into question the veracity of whatever Auld Tosh was about to say.

Regarding the etymology the DSL suggests that it is perhaps a conflation of English 'blabbe, A gurgling noise with the lips in a liquid and skellum, A worthless fellow, scamp, scoundrel, rogue, now sometimes used playfully to a young boy.'

Pauline Cairns Speitel

BOORACH *noun* a mound, an untidy heap

Boorach's etymology is in itself a right boorach. The Gaelic word *búrach* (a digging) appears in the DSL under the entry 'boorag', defined as a piece of turf used as peat or for roofing and illustrated by David Stephen in *Gleanings in the North* (1891) with this colourful quotation involving damage to daughter and dog: 'Maister Jolly, yin gigglegawkie, fat ye ca' m' son, dangs bowarag in my dochter's e'e, and tramped 'po' my folpey's feet'.[1]

Gaelic *búrach* comes from English *burrow* (a heap or mound), from Old English *beorg*. The dictionary is less clear on the derivation of boorach. It may be from *beorg*, but it has been suggested that it may be related to Old English *bur* (a dwelling) or *burg* (a fortified place), which gives us *burgh*. Whatever the source, we find it as a mound or a heap of stones in Alexander Gray's *Arrows* (1932): 'He has struck his fit on a bourock; he trippit and slippit, and syne He fell.' James Brown in *The Round Table Club* (1873) tells us: 'twenty deid deer waur coontit, a' lyin' in a boorach thegither.' John Black in *Melodies and Memories* (1909) describes seasonal cheer: 'O' holly leaves wi' berries bricht, An' bouracks big o' cake an' bun To grace the feasts an' spice the fun.'

Frequently, boorachs are untidy, hence the use of the word to describe a teenager's bedroom or, more figuratively, avant-garde music: 'a new-fangled music's juist a bourock' as TS Cairncross declares in the *Scots Magazine* (1928). In Mairi Hedderwick's *Katie Morag Delivers the Mail* (1997), Grannie says: 'Well, this is a fine boorach you've got yourself into, Katie Morag.' I know it as a crowd, huddle or cluster, like ES Rae in the *Banffshire Journal* (1920): 'An' boorichs black o' crawin' clamrin' craws.'

Chris Robinson

---

[1] *Master Jolly, is a silly person, is a name you would call my son, knocked a piece of turf in my daughter's eye, and stood on my dog's feet.*

BUCKIE *noun* the shell of a mollusc, an edible whelk

One of the earliest examples of buckie in the DSL comes from *The Historie of Scotland written first in Latin* by Johne Leslie and translated in Scottish by Father James Dalrymple (1596): 'In fresh water buckies… na lesse than in salt water buckies growis the margarite.'[1]

It possibly derives from the Latin *buccinum* (a whelk), which was used in dyeing to obtain the colour purple.

The edible little crustacean is remembered fondly by this Edinburgh native in the *Edinburgh Evening News* of 23 February 2008: 'We would spend it [pocket money] on mussels and buckies which looked like snails. The Newhaven fishwives would sell them on plates outside the pubs.' The Newhaven fishwives selling the buckies were also known as buckie wives as in this extract from *Close Encounters in the Royal Mile* (1997) by Alastair MR Hardie: 'Several other characters seen in the city streets… and a Newhaven fishwife – "The Buckie Wife" – who sat in the Lawnmarket in traditional dress beside a heavy wicker basket selling "portions of boiled whulks & buckies".'

However, it is also used figuratively to indicate shyness or lack of confidence so to encourage someone to be a bit more assertive one can urge them to 'come oot o their buckie', that is to come out of their shell. The following is from a 1936 Aberdeen source: 'He's a quare auld stock, bit he's fairly come oot o's buckie the nicht.'

On an even more up-to-date note, people can be encouraged to go into their shells but possibly not in the following example from the *Aberdeen Evening Express* of 19 September 2014: 'What happens now to those so desperate for independence? Do they simply disappear into their buckies and keep their heidies doon for another 50 years? I think not.'

Pauline Cairns Speitel

---

[1] *an archiac term for a pearl*

CADGER *noun* a hawker

Cadger is found in both Scots and English but its first documented appearance is in the translation of the *Aeneid* (1513) by Gavin Douglas: 'The cadgyar callis furth his capill wyth crakkis wail cant.'[1]

In England, both cadger and the verb cadge from which it derives seem to have a distinctly northern bias, and many of the quotations used by the OED are Scots. This distribution is borne out in place-name evidence. Although there is a Cadger Bank a little south of Newcastle, cadger does not appear frequently in English place-names, whereas Scotland has Cadger Burn, Cadgers Loan, Cadgers Loaning, Cadgers Brae and Cadgers Sheuch to remind us of the well-beaten paths of these itinerant salesman.

In the earlier Scots examples, the item for sale was predominantly fish. In Dunfermline in 1521, an old Act was sanctioned decreeing that cadgers 'sall present to the mercat oukly vj ladis of fysche.'[2] Sturgeon and porpoise were amongst the fish on offer as witnessed by *The Treasurer's Accounts* for 1512 which record the transport by cadgers of '1½ leid sture and pellok fische of Edinburgh to Carlile.'[3] No wonder the cadgers were also involved in the salt trade.

The *Report by Thomas Tucker upon the settlement of the revenues of excise and customs in Scotland* (1656) refers to 'Salt... which they usually sell to cageors... who carry the same about in creiles on horseback, or otherwise, up and downe the countrey.' Ramsay's *Collection of Proverbs* (1737) includes 'The King's Errand may come in the Cadger's Gate', implying that a great man may need the services of a humble one. An example is to be found in Donald MacLeod's *Past Worthies of the Lennox* (1894): 'I telt ye then that the day micht come when the king would come in the cadger's road, an' ye micht be gled o' a nicht's lodgin's frae me.'

Chris Robinson

---

[1] *The cadger summons his horse with very lively shouts.*

[2] *...shall present to the market weekly 6 ladis [ie the amount that can be carried on a horse] of fish*

[3] *One and a half loads of sturgeon and porpoise fish of Edinburgh to Carlisle*

CAIRD *noun* a tinker, a gypsy; a rough person

The origin of caird comes from Gaelic *ceard* and means a tinker or worker in metal. At what point it became a pejorative term for a gypsy is unclear.

It first appears in the DSL in Alexander Ross' *The Fortunate Shepherdess* (1768): 'He's either by the kairds or gypsies ta'en.' This example seems to imply that cairds and gypsies were two different sets of people who went around stealing children. (Why the myth took hold that gypsies stole the children of the settled population is lost to us.) Sir Walter Scott's *Heart of Midlothian* (1818) gives us a more neutral example: 'This fellow had been originally a tinkler, or caird, many of whom stroll about these districts.'

However, by 1894, SR Crockett's *Raiders* leaves us in no doubt what the word had come to mean: 'A set of wild cairds – cattle reivers and murderers.'

To be caird-tongued was 'to be given to loose talk' and the DSL has evidence of this from informants in the Aberdeenshire area in the 1930s. A late 20th century example also from the North East and not necessarily describing a gypsy, comes from David Kerr Cameron's *The Ballad and the Plough* (1978): 'There is, it is true, 'Kempie' the grieve of 'The Barns o' Beneuches', a caird-tongued (rough-spoken) man whose constant seiging (raging) finally leads to his own dismissal...'

Finally, in *An Anthology of New Celtic Writing* edited by Anne Cameron (1995), we have an example of the original meaning: 'They refused to learn English or any language but their own, they refused to put their children in school to be educated in Scaldie[1] ways or taught Scaldie manners. And so the Scaldies, for the good of the Cairds of course, gathered them up and transported them away from the land they had known since the days of Fergus...'

Pauline Cairns Speitel

---

[1] *Scaldies is the name Travellers gave to the settled population. 'Scaldie ways' would be used to describe an ability to fit in and conform with the non-travelling community.*

CAPERCAILZIE *noun* the wood-grouse

Whether you pronounce the first syllable as 'cap' or 'cape' is up to you, but don't pronounce that 'z'. It represents the letter 'yogh', pronounced like the first sound in 'yes' but usually silent in capercailzie, as the spellings in these quotations suggest. Not only does the capercailzie have an interesting spelling, it also has an interesting derivation from the Gaelic *capull coille* meaning 'horse of the wood' in reference to its considerable size. The male bird measures 33 inches. James Dalrymple, in his translation of Leslie's *Historie of Scotland* (1596) writes: 'A certane foul and verie rare called the capercalze to name with the vulgar peple, the horse of the forrest.'

In 1746, T Oliphant's *The Jacobite Lairds of Gask* claims, 'Caperkellies are frequently sold in mercat' but, by 1760, Robert Popcocke in *Tours in Scotland* notes: 'In the Mountain towards Fort Augustus they have found the Caper Keily (Cock of the Wood). They are now very rare. I saw the skin of one stuffed, they are about the size of a Turkey, the head like a Grouse or Moor Fowl, entirely black, except that the Belly is spotted with White, and it is white under the Wings.' The 1795 *Statistical Account* laments: 'The caper coille, or wild turkey, was seen in Glenmoriston, and in the neighbouring district of Strathglass, about 40 years ago, and it is not known that this bird has appeared since, or that it now exists in Britain.'

It was reintroduced from Sweden in the late 1830s and once more 'The capercailzie up the glen Was churkin' loodly to his hen' (A Rea, *The Divot Dyke*, 1898). This quotation does not do justice to the call which starts as a rattle and then sounds disconcertingly like the popping of a cork and pouring of liquid, ending with a harsh grinding noise.

Chris Robinson

CARLIN, CARLINE *noun* a disparaging term for an old woman; a witch

Carlin or carline is another very old Scots contemptuous term for a woman. In the DSL, the first example comes from the *Legends of the Saints* (1380): 'Fra he herde the karling mak Sa fare hicht, he can confort tak.'

From the late 14th century, it continued its journey into the 'modern' language with this example from the DSL taken from J Arbuthnot's *John Bull* published in 1712: 'Then there's no living with that old carline his mother; she rails at Jack, and Jack's an honester man than any of her kin.' One can only feel sorry for the poor, scolded Jack but perhaps he hadn't tidied his room. JM Barrie in his *Farewell Miss Julie Logan* first published in the *Times* of 24 December 1931 seems only to mean that a woman is elderly: 'It was eerie to reflect that to those two carlines, as we call ancient women, my study must still be more his than mine.'

However, carlin is familiar to us today because of a poet from Ayrshire called Robert Burns. In his epic poem *Tam o' Shanter*, which he penned in 1790, Burns beautifully captures a picture of a witch with the following description of witches partying: 'They reel'd, they set, they cross'd, they cleekit, Till ilka carlin swat and reekit.'

Finally, the following is from a poem entitled *My Granny* from s4 pupil Allanna Barron published in *The Herald* of 25 April 1995: 'Oor Granny's a carline my sister says.'

Pauline Cairns Speitel

CARNAPTIOUS, CURNAPTIOUS *adjective* bad-tempered, irritable, quarrelsome

We Scots it seems have many descriptive terms for negative personality traits. Some unkind people might argue that the Scottish personality deserves some of these terms. One of the more descriptive is carnaptious and just saying it conjures up an image of an irascible, usually male, person.

Its origins are unclear but the OED suggests that it could be a form of English *captious* which has a similar meaning and gives its roots as Scottish and Irish dialect. OED also has the earliest attestation from the *Ulster Journal of Archaeology* of 1858: 'A nivver seen wan so curnaptious.'

The DSL also has examples from Ulster Scots, the following is from WG Lyttle's *Readings by Robin* from 1879: 'He's a cross carnapshus wee brat, so he is!'

The first Scottish example comes from *Curdies* by HS Robertson and is from Glasgow in 1931: 'That belangt to ane they ca'd Rab Frew, a carnaptious auld deevil he was.'

The first 21st century example comes from *The Herald* of 28 September 2000: 'It's said that when a rescue ship reached a remote desert island, the crew were astounded to discover that a single survivor of the shipwreck, a carnaptious Scotsman, had built two churches – one to attend, and one to stay away from on principle.'

Carnaptious is such a powerfully descriptive term that it is still regularly used by journalists today: 'To put this in context though, Brian Wilson, the carnaptious hammer of Scottish independence, was once himself a nationalist.' (*The Herald*, 2 May 2016).

Pauline Cairns Speitel

CHORE, CHORIE *verb* to steal, **CHOR** *noun* a thief

'Chore' or 'chorie' was originally a word used by Scottish gypsies and travellers. The first record in the DSL dates from 1911 with a reference to *The Scotsman* of 23 December. However, Walter Simson writing in 1865, recorded the forms 'chor' and 'tschor' and gives the example: 'I asked her to leave this place fearing that her chavie[1] was a chor.' This meaning seems to have been only used by gypsies and the modern noun meaning would usually be used in the phrase 'on the chore' as the following extract from an anti-burglary poem in the *Scottish Daily Mail* of 10 April 2015 shows: 'Staying in or goin oot? Lock the windaes 'n' front door. A simple step maybe, that'll prevent access tae them on the chore.' The following quotation from Irving Welsh's *Marabou Stork Nightmares* (1995) shows the use of the verb in the language of the non-gypsy population: 'They must have thought we were gaunny chorie aypils[2] or something.'

At what point and in what way, or why, many of these originally traveller or gypsy words came to be used by the general Scots-speaking population is unclear. It has been suggested by authors of traveller origin – Betsy Whyte and Jess Smith – that the reason many of these words were used by children was because traveller children had to attend mainstream schools for a certain number of days a year and, naturally, took their language with them.

The DSL gives the etymology as coming from Romany *chor, choar* (to steal). Further research suggests a connection to Hindi or Sanskrit which have the words *chor* and *chora* respectively with the same meaning.

Pauline Cairns Speitel

---

[1] *son*
[2] *apples*

CLABBYDHU *noun* a large mussel

Scotland, famous for its seafood, gives the above name for an amazingly large mussel. The suggested etymology aptly derives it from Gaelic *clab* meaning an enormous mouth and *dubh* meaning black or dark.

The word is not recorded in the DSL until comparatively recently. From 1850, we have an original declaration of love in D Macilreavie's *Flory Loynachan*: 'O, the Clabbydhu, it loves the Trinch, The Crouban (crab), the quay-neb (the point o the quay)... But, Flory, I love thee!' Yet, as early as 1909, there is a hint of their decline in James Colville's *Studies in Lowland Scots* where he defines the clabbydhu as a 'Black bivalve, a large mussel still quite familiar on the lower Clyde estuary.' James Bridie in a letter (1940) writes: 'a clabbydoo is a coarse type of clam found on Loch Fyne side. It is shaped roughly like an oyster and buries itself in sandy shingle. It is edible only when it has been boiled.'

More modern quotations show that they are still being eaten, and very tasty they are. In Christine Marion Fraser's *Children of Rhanna* (1983), we find the tempting invitation: '"Will you be havin' a clappy doo wi' me, lassie?" he asked, indicating a driftwood fire on which sat a can filled to the brim with large mussels.' In 1987, Peter Mason's *C'mon Geeze Yer Patter!* (1987), a shopping list consists of '2 punna aipples, Hauf-a-dizzen tattie scones, A jaur a clappy doos, 2 boatles a ginger and A punna mince.' It seems that the word and its variants ('clockiedow', 'cluggie-dhu', 'clappiedoo') may also be applied to the inedible but pearl-bearing freshwater horse-mussel. However, meat and pearls are not the only things you can find in a mussel as witnessed by this curious quotation from W Cramond in *Reminiscences of the Old Town of Cullen* (1810): 'Cerat'sa' to heal wounds was supplied in a mussel shell.'[1]

Chris Robinson

---

[1] *Cerat is a type of stiff oitment and 'sa' is the Scots for English* salve

COLLIE BUCKIE *noun* a piggy-back ride

There are many descriptions of piggy-back or pick-a-back rides in the DSL but the most common of these is collie-buckie or coalie backie which indicates that the term comes from the similarity of a 'coal porter' carrying a bag of coal on his back.

The sparsity of written records is because in essence this come from children's language and children's games which by their very nature were rarely written down except for specialist collectors, such as the writer James TR Ritchie in his *Golden City* published in 1965 which documents Edinburgh children's street games, and I & P Opie who documented children's games throughout the United Kingdom in their work *Children's Games* published in 1969 which recorded *collie back* from Aberdeen and Edinburgh.

In the DSL, many variations of *collie buckie* are documented so we have: *coalie back* from an informant in Argyllshire; from Selkirk in 1975, we have *collie-cod*; and Edinburgh informants in the 1990s gave us both *collie buckie* and *coalie backie*. One scarce written example comes from John Byrne's *The Slab Boys* (1987): 'Hector had to give him a coalie-back down the stairs.' A 21st century written example comes from the *Edinburgh Evening News* of 20 August 2002: '...as he gave them coalie buckie rides on his back.'

Children also turned *collie buckies* into a rough boys' game called a 'collie buckie fight' which, according to the DSL, involved 'a jostling or jousting by children mounted on the back of others, a pick-a-back fight.'

Pauline Cairns Speitel

CONVOY *verb* to accompany

I was reminded of this original use of convoy when a male friend offered me his arm 'to convoy ye doon the road'. On examining this in the DSL, I found that indeed this usage is Scots and is given the following definition: 'To escort, accompany, conduct (without any idea of armed protection). This sense has now died out in English.'

On checking the DSL, I found that this meaning goes back to 1375 and Barbour's *Bruce*: 'Till the men off Northummyrland Suld cum armyt, and… Conwoy hym till hys cuntre'[1] although this example sounds as if the person is being convoyed a wee bit further than 'doon the road'.

Moving into the 'modern' period, Boswell's *London Journal* of 1763 has the following example: 'He convoyed me up Snow Hill as far as to Cheapside.'

There are also many up-to-date examples in the DSL which seem to begin in the early 20th century. From Aberdeen in the 1920 work, *In Country Places* by Charles Murray: 'The fite-fuskered cat wi' her tail in the air Convoyed him as far as the barn.' At the other end of the 20th century, the following comes from Aberdeen's *Press and Journal* of 4 July 1992: 'To convoy somebody is so much couthier than accompany. I still go for a traivel rather than a walk.'

And into the 21st century James Robertson in his novel from the year 2000, *The Fanatic*, gives us: 'I was at the Netherbow Port, inspecting the guard and now I am on my way to a prayer-meeting. I would be obliged if ye'd convoy me to the Grassmarket.'

Pauline Cairns Speitel

---

[1] *To the men of Northumberland should come armed, and… convoy him to his country.*

DAIDLE *noun* a bib or pinafore

Daidle or daidlie is rather long-windedly defined in the DSL as: 'A pinafore, a cloth put on the breast of a child, to keep it clean during the time of eating, a larger sort of bib.'

Although this word is marked as obsolescent in the DSL, one of our informants reminded us of it as recently as June 2017.

Examples in the DSL seem to describe an apron as in the following from DJ Beattie's *Oor Gate-en'* published in 1915: 'In the distance micht be seen, here and there, the pink an white dadles o' the bairns getherin blaeberries.' However, the following example from John Firth's *Reminiscences of an Orkney Parish* (1920) describing how children were dressed seems to indicate a pinafore: 'The plain gown of printed cotton or wincey reached almost to the ankles, and over it was worn a small square apron, the 'fented dedley' (gored pinafore) only coming into fashion later.'

The pinafore seems to have been worn by children of both sexes as in the memories of a man writing in the *Aberdeen People's Journal* of February 1863: '...but especially the days when I was a wee callant with a daidly at Dominie Duncan school...'

Into the 1930s, daidlies were still known in the compound 'daidly-apron' which seems to have been a much more heavy-duty canvas apron.

As with many Scots words, the etymology is unclear but the DSL suggests it may come from the English dialect word 'dowly' (a washing rag).

Pauline Cairns Speitel

DEVAL *verb* to descend, decline, cease

The DSL is not short of dreich and dowie alliteration using the letter 'd'. Gavin Douglas' *Aeneid* (1513) offers 'the day [began] to dyrkyn, declyne, and devaill'. John Rolland's *Court of Venus* (c1550) has 'Thy dolf hart for dredour ay deuaillis'. Less poetically, and in somewhat limited use, we find it meaning to travel downstream as in David Calderwood's *History of the Kirk of Scotland* (a1651): 'They tooke boat the secund of June, and devailed toward a shipp.'

Deval comes from Old French *devaler* or *devaller* meaning 'to go or let down', which accords well with these earlier quotations. The commonest modern sense is to cease, stop or leave off and this is first recorded in the 16th century romance, *Clariodus*: 'Fra laughter then ilk ane could neer devall'.

Since then, we find it in the comparatively formal setting of a letter by Sir Walter Scott (1827): 'Except about three or four hours for food and exercise I have not till today devaled from my task.' and in the conversational tones of John Galt's *Ayrshire Legatees* (1821): 'Becky, will you never devawl wi' your backbiting.' Donald A Mackenzie in a letter of 1933 puts it in a thoroughly domestic setting: 'Devall was common in my boyhood. When youngsters made a noise, grannie would exclaim, "Bairns, bairns, will ye no devall?"' In some instances, a final, unetymological 'd' has been added. This may have occurred as a hypercorrection. As the 'd' is often not pronounced in words like 'auld' and 'cauld', some writers may, by analogy, have restored a 'd' that never was. The follow-on is that other people come along and think that if it is written down it must be true and pronounce it accordingly. This spelling is used by WD Latto in *Tammas Bodkin* (1864): 'His tongue gaed like the clapper o' a kail bell withoot devald.'

Chris Robinson

DICHT *verb* to wipe, clean, put in good order

Nowadays, dicht is usually used in the sense of to wipe. The Aberdeen Makar, Sheena Blackhall, uses it frequently. In *The Bonsai Grower* (1998), we read of mothers 'dichtin bibbly snoots'. In the DSL, it is still found in related senses such as to polish, clean or sweep. *Edinburgh Burgh Records* (1530) note the requirement that 'euery man and woman dicht and mak clene befor ther durris[1] and closis'. Stirling's defences were well cared for, because the *Burgh Records* (1651) contain an entry 'For thrie sheep skins to dight the cannon'.

The parent Old English word *dihtan* had a wider range of meanings, several of which were shared by Scots and English until the word became obsolete in English in the 16th century. It often meant to dress or decorate. Robert Henryson in the late 15th century describes a magnificent 'croun of massie gold… With… mony diueris dyamontis dicht.'[2]

According to the lexicographer, John Jamieson (1808): 'A discourse is said to be weil dicht, when the subject is well handled.'

Dicht could also mean to sift or winnow grain and, in Angus, in the mid-20th century, a strong wind could still be described as 'A wind at wid dicht bere'.[3] Food can also be dichtit, hence a hospitable proverb from David Fergusson's collection (1641): 'A friend's dinner is soon dight.' Another proverb drew upon the habit that hens have of wiping their beaks before going to roost. So, we get this political comment from James Ballantine's *The Gaberlunzie's Wallet* (1843): 'Wha's to be prime minister say ye? Charlie Fox? Troth man, that's good news indeed… Troth an' Billie Pitt may now e'en dight his neb and flee up.' If you want to tell someone in Scots to take a look at themselves before criticising others, you might say 'Dicht yer ain door stane'.

Chris Robinson

---

[1] *doors*

[2] *…many diverse diamonds dicht*

[3] *barley*

DINGIE, DINGY *verb* to rebuff, to ignore, fail to keep a (romantic) appointment

Dingie (pronounced with the 'ing' as in sing) is a recently recorded addition to Scottish Language Dictionaries' word research and will be added to the revised editions of our dictionaries. I think the best informal translation would be the colloquial English phrase 'to knock back'.

Dingie is a derivation of the Scots 'ding' which is defined in the DSL as 'To knock, beat or strike: to drive; to push suddenly and forcibly; to displace or overturn by shoving' and the very earliest example of 'ding' in the DSL comes from the *Legends of the Saints* by John Barbour (1380): 'With stanys gert men his mouth dinge.'

The first written example of the modern 'dingie' comes from *The Dictionary of Playground Slang* by Chris Lewis (2003) and he defines it as follows: 'to stand some up or ignore them... Used as "He pure dingied me, by the way..." Circa 1980s-current (Scot).' How he knows it was current in the 1980s, however, he does not say. The next piece of evidence was from oral informants from Edinburgh in 2006 and 2009 respectively. One is from a schoolboy which would fit in with Chris Lewis' findings but the other is from an adult woman.

All the examples so far found are from the 21st century and the most recent was used by Gary: Tank Commander (the alter ego of comedian Greg McHugh) when he interviewed First Minister Nicola Sturgeon and asked her if she would 'dingy Donald Trump' to which the First Minister replied that: 'America will dingy Donald Trump before I do!'

Pauline Cairns Speitel

DISJASKIT adjective dejected, downcast, neglected, weary

If you are dejected and weary after the bitter winter, here is the word for you. This heartfelt example of our word in action in the DSL comes from Violet Jacob's *More Songs of Angus* (1918): 'I'm fairly disjaskit, Christina, The warld an' its glories are toom.'

Disjaskit can also mean neglected, untidy or dilapidated. The character created by James Smith in Jenny Blair's *Maunderings* (1872) might have been quite joco[1] for all we know: 'An auld yellow cotton rag that he dignifies wi' the name o' a Sunday shirt! – the disjasket-lookin' crater!' Another dishevelled individual appears in this eloquent put-down from SR Crockett's *The Grey Man* (1896): 'Keep your ill tongue for that disjaskit, ill-put-thegither rachle o' banes that ye hae for guidman.'

In Sir Walter Scott's *Old Mortality* (1816), we read: 'Tak the first broken disjasked-looking road that makes for the hills.' Poor highway maintenance is nothing new, apparently.

A strange, sad example is found in George Macdonald's *Alec Forbes of Howglen* (1865): '...for sic a throuither disjaskit midden o' lere, I never saw,'[2] Some quotations used in the DSL to illustrate the sense of weary are slightly ambiguous and are not completely severed from the other senses of untidy or dejected. One example, however, from the *New Shetlander* (1947) does clearly evoke the backbreaking exhaustion of harvest labour: 'Dedzjaskit, a hairst time, wi' kruklin ta shaer.' Where straightforward tiredness is involved, the related word forjaskjit is more common, as in Walter Elliot's *Clash-ma-clavers*: 'An, fair forjaskit, he lay doun Tae tak a roadside nap.' To return to disjaskit, we hope we have not, like the writer in Tait's *Edinburgh Magazine* (1835), 'got intil a bad habit o' writing lang disjasket sort o' sentences.'

Chris Robinson

---

[1] *jovial, cheerful*

[2] *for such a muddled, dilapidated rubbish heap of a face, I never saw.*

DIZZY *noun* a rejection. *verb* to reject; fail to keep a (romantic) appointment

In these days of instant communication, I don't know if the situation of 'getting a dizzy' or being 'stood up' can still happen but being 'dizzied' or being stood up was a humiliating situation for persons of both sexes.

The first example in the DSL is from 1958 in Cliff Hanley's autobiographical *Dancing in the Street* where he cites the plight of some poor, rejected friends: 'Sometimes people who hadn't been able to get into the pictures or who had been dissied by girl-friends, came up to sit at the fire and talk.' Peter Mason, nearly 30 years later in his glossary, specifically of Glasgow speech, *C'mon Geeze yer Patter* (1987), gives the example: 'Ah wis black affronted gittin a dissy at Boots' coarner.'

Michael Munro in his collection *The Complete Patter* (1996) gives both example and definition: 'If you make a date with someone and then fail to turn up you are said to have given that person a dizzy: "What's up son, did the lemon curd (burd) gie ye a dizzy?"' He also gives the same suggested etymology as the DSL saying that it is likely a shortening of disappointment.

However, getting a dizzy does not only happen in the west. Research at Scottish Language Dictionaries gives this Edinburgh example: 'Ah wis dizzied at Binn's Corner.' In Edinburgh's West End, the corner site of this department store (now Fraser's) was a popular place for trysts.

Dizzy Corner as mentioned above in Peter Mason's example does still seem to be current in the collective memory of Glaswegians: 'Most Glaswegians still call it Dizzy Corner, the spot where, in gentler times, stood-up youngsters waited for their missing dates under the clock at Boots.'

Pauline Cairns Speitel

DOUP, DOWP *noun* bottom part (of something)

The earliest recorded use is in the compound 'e-dolp' meaning eye-socket. This first example appears in Gavin Douglas' translation of the *Aeneid* (1513): 'Off his E dolp the flowand blude and attir[1] He wysch away.' Other examples refer to the bottom of eggshells. In Fergusson's *Proverbs* (1641), we are told 'Better half egge nor toome[2] doupe.' Walter Gregor in *Notes on the Folk-Lore of the North-East of Scotland* (1881) gives tips on poultry husbandry: 'That all the birds might be hatched much about the same time the eggs were put below the hen all at once... with the words... "A've set a hen wi' nine eggs; Muckle luck amon hir legs. Doups an shalls gang ower the sea, Cocks an hens come hame t' me."' Here's hoping that not too many 'died in the dowp' or expired before hatching. Folklore has it that witches went to sea in egg dowps and William Scott picks up on this notion in a poem of 1832 where they can 'Transform a ploughman to a horse to prance, An' sail in egg-doups to the coast o' France.'

Dowp can also mean the buttocks and dowp-scud refers to a painful impact on that part of the anatomy. One wonders what terpsichorean antics Aberdeen Town Council got up to that made it necessary for this prayer of 1811 in a *Garland of Bon Accord*: 'God prosper lang our Lord Provost Town Clerk, an' Baillies a'; An' grant that i' their reeling fits[3], Doup-scud they minna fa'.'

The seat of the trousers, or dowp of the breeks, make several appearances in the dictionaries. James Hogg in *Jacobite Relics* (1819) makes reference to 'A pair o' breeks that wants the doup'. In fact, dowp can mean the bottom end of just about anything, including candles and cigarettes.

Chris Robinson

---

[1] *pus*
[2] *empty*
[3] *dances*

DUX *noun* top pupil in a class

Dux, Latin for 'leader', is a term used in Scotland for the top pupil in a class, subject or school.

The earliest example in the DSL comes from the *Scots Magazine* of August 1799: 'The examination of the High School took place on the 13th. The gold medal was given to master Rollo, as dux of the first class.' (I wonder if the medal was real gold.)

Coming in as runner-up also had its own title of second dux as in this example from EB Ramsay's *Reminiscences of Scottish Life and Character* from 1867: '"I'm second dux..." means in Scottish academical language second from the top of the class.'

The most modern citation in the DSL is from 1937 in the *St Andrews Citizen*: 'Prizes to Dux in French, Dux in Greek, and Dux in English Essay.'

There is then a leap to 1990 and an example from the novel *Bannock* by Ian McGinness: 'He showed off Stannie's report cards in the club, and when the boy finished primary school his Dux medal was placed on the largest table in the bar for on glorious night of celebration.'

I thought this a rather old-fashioned term long consigned to the history books and the reminiscences of our parents and grandparents. I should know better. Lexicographers should never 'dagger' something (mark as obsolete) unless absolutely certain – which of course, in reality, we can never be.

Witness the following examples from the late 20th and 21st centuries: 'A pair of bright sparks have booked their place in the history books after coming top of the class. Primary 7 pupils Craig Mason and Christine Milne have been named duxes of Woodside Primary School, Aberdeen.' Craig and Christine's moment of fame was reported in *The Aberdeen Evening Express* of 29 June 1998. Incidentally, the plural should, I think, be duces.

There are many examples from this century including this recent one from the *Daily Record* of 4 July 2016: 'Bethany Reid completed a unique family hat-trick when she was named this year's dux medallist at Airdrie Academy.' Bethany's gran and brother had also had the same honour.

Pauline Cairns Speitel

DWAM *noun* a swoon, a trance. v*erb* to swoon, decline in health

Dwams can range from an indication of a serious illness to a pleasant daydream. William Dunbar uses it, with some hyperbole as he lived to tell the tale, in a poem of unrequited love from the early 16th century: 'Sic deidlie dwawmes... Ane hundrithe tymes hes my hairt ouirpast.' Despite appearances, the dwam in this song (1724) by Lady G Baillie is not fatal either, but merely a delaying tactic by the groom's mother: 'The day it was set, and the bridal to be, The wife took a dwam, and lay down to die'.

Some dwams, in the sense of fainting fits are short-lived but others signal a more prolonged decline, as shown in Ian Maclaren's *Beside the Bonnie Brier Bush* (1894): 'He begood to dwam in the end of the year and soughed awa in the spring.'[1] This strange symptom described in SR Crockett's *The Stickit Minister* (1893) might puzzle the doctor: 'She has been troubled wi' a kin o' dwaminess in her inside for near three weeks.'

James Smith's account of Jenny Blair's *Maunderings* (1872) illustrates that some dwams have pleasant romantic origins: 'Then she gangs to her bed in a saft, dwamy condition, an' dreams a' the nicht o' the words that had kittled her lug sae finely.' Other dwams have more prosaic causes, such as this from John Service's *Dr Duguid* (1887): 'She was in a dwaam of drink.'

Animals, too, are affected by the occasional dwam. We have a pig giving cause for concern in CP Slater's *Marget Pow* (1925): 'Every now and then she keeked out, hopin' the pig was only in a dwalm.' By contrast, and showing the use of dwam as a verb, Sheena Blackhall in *Wittgenstein's Web* (1996) describes a contented cat: 'Sylvester wis curled up inno a cosy baa, dwaumin o Fuskers an cream.'

Chris Robinson

---

[1] *He began to decline in health at the end of the year and died in the spring.*

ELDRITCH *adjective* weird, uncanny

Possibly this word comes from Old English *elfrice*, literally 'elf-kingdom' and most of the contexts in which we find it certainly suggest other worlds. We have it explicitly linked with 'elf' in William Stewart's metrical version of Boece's history (1535): 'Thinkand it war sum elrische man or elfe.' The Bellenden translation of Boece (1531) uses it of three kenspeckle witches: 'Makbeth and Banquho... met be the gait thre wemen, clothit in elrage and uncouth weid',[1] but the best-known example comes from Burns' *Tam o' Shanter* (1793): 'So Maggie runs, the witches follow, Wi' monie an eldritch skriech and hollo.'

Many writers link it with Pluto and incubi. This quotation from William Dunbar's *Golden Targe* (a1508) is typical: 'Thare was Pluto, the elrich incubus, In cloke of grene.' Grene, of course, is closely associated with elves or fairies, and eldritch fairies appear in David Lindsay's *Ane Satyre of the Thrie Estaits* (1540): 'I pray the alreche quene of fary To be your protectioun.' Gavin Douglas in his Aeneidos (1513) uses 'Tha elrych bredyr' in reference to the Cyclops, warning us 'All is bot gaistis, and elrich fastasyis, Of browneis and of bogillis ful this buke.'

Tourists in Edinburgh might be wary of the lower part of the Royal Mile if they read Allan Ramsay's *Poems* (1721): 'O Cannigate! poor elritch hole, What Loss, what Crosses does thou thole!'

Helen W Pryde creates a noun to use with comic effect in *McFlannel Family Affairs* (1950): 'And as the scraighs[2] rose in pitch and volume there was added to the eldritchery the terror shrieks of Sarah and the bewitched yapping of Susan the dog', but the eldritchery is really no laughing matter; as the poet Charles Fleming chillingly reminds us in *Poems, Songs and Essays* (1878), 'time's a chiel that stan's wi' eldrich whittle'.[3]

Chris Robinson

---

[1] *clothing*

[2] *shrieks*

[3] *time is a child that stands with eldritch knife*

ETTLE *verb* to intend, plan, aim

This word comes from Old Norse *ætla* and makes its first appearance in Scots around 1400 in John Barbour's *Troy Book*. On balance, ettlin in the DSL seems predominantly directed towards mischief but this bias could be because of splendid examples from court records. The *Council Register of the Burgh of Aberdeen* alone gives us: 'He... drew furth his dager, aitling to hawe strukin the said officier thairwith' (1605) and, involving an unusual weapon, 'For etling to strik the said Issobell with ane brasin pan' (1643).

The sense sometimes drifts into 'aim' as in A Ross' late 18th century *Fortunate Shepherd*: 'A gentle squire of freely gentle cast, Of sweet address, an' skill'd in courting art, That well coud ettle Cupid's winning dart', hence J Kelly's *Proverbs* (1721): 'Oft Etle, whiles hit. This he explains as; "People who have made many Tryals to do a Thing, may hit right at last."'

Burns uses it as a noun in *Tam o' Shanter* in which 'Nannie... flew at Tam wi' furious ettle' and this determined declaration comes from James Stewart's *Sketches o Scottish Character* (1857): 'An' I winna be put frae my ettle, Not e'en by auld Hornie himsel'. A similar determination lies behind this ambitious imperative from John Galt's *The Provost*: 'Ye're ettling at the magistracy... and I'll no let ye rest if ye dinna mak' me a bailie's wife or a' be done.'

A more modest and understandable desire is expressed in P Macgillivray's *Bog-Myrtle and Peat Reek* (1922): 'An' aye we ettle't the ither dram, Wi' dry oatcakes for a foond.'[1] To end on a thoughtful note, here is a sentiment from JL Waugh's *Robbie Doo* (1910): 'Hope! ay, it's the ettler o' youth and the solace o' age: lose it, and the first's a failure and the last a burden.'

Chris Robinson

---

[1] *foundation*

FANKLE *noun* a tangle, a muddle *verb* to tangle, muddle, twist

Fankle is derived from fank, meaning a coil of rope, or to twist or tangle. Fankles or fankling can be physical, as in this quotation from Robin Jenkins' *Fergus Lamont* (1979): 'She spoiled every game she took part in[...] if it was skipping ropes she got them fankled round her neck'; or this from Jimmy Boyle's *Hero of the Underworld* (1999): 'Having given me a rapid introduction to animal innards, he accurately tossed the trespassing hearts or lungs or whatever to their rightful tanks. I, meantime, found myself slithering in a fankle of intestines.'

Figurative uses include this 1995 example from Chris Dolan's *Poor Angels*: 'He'd suggested she go to her Mum's – where she always went when she got into one of her fankles...' and this rather more philosophical example spoken by a character in Robin Jenkins' *The Thistle and the Grail* (1994): 'But human affairs aye get into a fankle.'

As we can see from the DSL life in times gone by was beset by fankles and fankling too, with the verb forms appearing before the noun ones. The earliest referred specifically to being caught in a snare. For example, in 1724, Allan Ramsay in his collection of poems *Ever Green*, tells of 'Our Royal Lord [Quha] now is fast heir fanklet in a cord', and the following 1788 example cited in the *Scots Magazine* uses fank in a similar sense: 'And thoch I'm fankit i' my tether, And darna thole ilk kind o' weather.'

Fankle can also mean to stumble, as illustrated by this quote from *Dr Duguid* by John Service (1887): 'Her auld guidman as he cam warplin' an' fanklin' owre the muirs.' You may well say 'Nae wunner ma mind's in a fankle' (from the *Bellshill Speaker*, 1923).

Ann Ferguson

FERNTICKLE *noun a* freckle

Ferntickles are a matter of taste and, while I find them rather attractive, most of the authors quoted in the DSL and its supplements emphatically do not. Some quotations set them alongside other disfigurements such as skin eruptions. In the *Edinburgh Evening Courant* (1772), a woman is described as 'About the age of 22, between fair and brown complexion, fairn-tickled, her face somewhat foul, and small plooks about the brow.' John Buchan did not mean to draw a pretty picture in *Witch Wood* (1927) of 'Yon body wi' the fernietickles and the bleary een.'

Perhaps coined as a reference to the brown spores of ferns, it is first found in the *Catholicon Anglicum* (1483), an English-Latin wordbook, where it is glossed as 'lenticula', a word literally meaning 'lentil-shaped' but also used in the sense of 'freckle' by Pliny the Elder. Perhaps the Roman sun brings out larger ferntickles.

William Turner's *A New Herball* (1551) recommends vinegar for their removal, and Thomas D'Urfy in *Wit and Mirth: or Pills to Purge Melancholy* (1791) introduces his readers to 'Pluggy fac'd Wat... And... farnicled Huggy' but, thereafter, the word seems to disappear from English and only survives in the Scots language of Scotland and Ulster.

A Glossary of Words in Use in the Counties of Antrim and Down (1880) by WH Patterson contains the proverb 'The farntickles niver sayd a word but one, that they wouldn't light on a din[1] skin.' Indeed, ferntickles and the fair complexion of a redhead go together, as in Charles Murray's *Sough o' War* (1917): 'A roch reid-heidit bairn, wi' ferny-tickled nose.' There is something endearing about that wean and a compliment to the lady seems intended in the *Northern Whig and Belfast Post* (1931): 'Wilson is a bit gurly,[2] but he has a farn-tickled, sonsy daughter.'

Chris Robinson

---

[1] *dun colour*
[2] *bad-tempered*

FIRST FIT *noun* the first person to enter a house in the New Year

First-footing is one of the best known Scottish New Year customs. In RH Cromek's *Remains of Nithsdale and Galloway Song* (1810), we learn 'Much care is taken that the persons who enter be what are called sonsie folk, for on the admission of the first-foot depends the prosperity or trouble of the year.'

According to *The Reminiscences of the Ferguslie Elderly Forum* (1993): 'You always wanted someone dark to first foot you and they had to have a bit of coal and a bun, currant bun or shortbread.' An earlier quotation from Ebenezer Picken's *A Dictionary of the Scottish Language* (1818) claims: 'The first-fit generally carries with him a hot beverage, made of ale, spirits, eggs, cream, sugar, and biscuit, with some slices of curran bun to be eaten along with it, or perhaps some bread and cheese.' Different times and areas favour their own offerings, including salt and whisky, but the lump of coal, once common, is rarer in the absence of open fires. Physical attributes are important. Robert Ford in *Humorous Scotch Readings* (1881) illustrates two undesirable traits: 'He was a fair-hair'd, flet-fitted man, an' therefore, an unlucky first-fit.'

Few people now realise that a first fit could also be the first person (or sometimes animal) met on any journey, especially on the way to church by a wedding or christening party. Walter Gregor in *An Echo of the Olden Time* (1874) records: 'The person first met [by bridal procession] received a glass, with bread and cheese, and then turned and walked a short distance. Great attention was paid to the first fit. A man on horseback, or a horse drawing a cart... was deemed most lucky.' Did the horse get its share of the bread and cheese?

Chris Robinson

FLEG *verb* to frighten; *noun* a fright

Fleg makes its earliest appearance in the DSL with a quotation from James Melvill's *Autobiography and Diary* (1600): 'When courtlie wolffes from Chrystes flok be flegged.' The only other example of the word in this dictionary is the comforting assertion in Pitcairn's *Criminal Trials* (1662) that 'The Lord fleigged the Feind with his holy candles.'

In the post-1700 period covered by the *Scottish National Dictionary*, the word really comes into its own both as a verb and as a noun, and it is even used to form the adjective 'flegsome' and the agent noun 'flegger'. Not surprisingly, several quotations relate to hauntings past, present and yet to come. J Duff, in *A Collection of Poems* (1816), warns 'Some think his ghaist still haunts Glendevon, To fleig the wives wha gae to Methven' and in G Macdonald's *Sir Gibbie* (1879) the threat is made that 'I'll wrastle frae my grave an' fleg ye oot o' the sma' wuts ye hae, my man,'[1]

Some other quotations, however, show the word in a more positive, figurative light, in the sense of chasing away such unwanted things as a sore, husky throat, as the poet Robert Fergusson suggests: 'To fleg frae a' your craigs the roup, Wi' reeking het and crieshy soup',[2] or extremes of cold as Charles Murray advises in *In the Country Places* (1920): 'Haud on the peats an' fleg the cauld.'

Still, fleg for the most part retains a sense of fear and alarm such as we find in the claim made in Neil Munro's *Doom Castle* (1901) that 'We gied the English a fleg at the "Forty-five".' The Scots are made of sterner stuff though; the *St Andrews Citizen* (28 January 1939) says, 'They canna' fleg the couthie folk that bide frae John-o-Groats Down to the Mull o' Galloway.'

Chris Robinson

---

[1] *I'll struggle from my grave and frighten you out of the little wit you have, my man.*

[2] *To frighten from all your throats the infection, With steaming hot and greasy soup*

FURRY BOOTS CITY *noun* a nickname for Aberdeen

The first example of this Aberdonian nickname shown in the DSL comes from *The Herald* of 24 July 1992: 'Going to Nuremberg to drive and talk about Audis had undertones of Tom Shields' Furry Boots City.' Later that same year in *The Independent* of 30 November, the meaning was extended to Aberdeen's football team as in: 'The men from the furry boots city are beginning to draw attention... having scored 13 goals in their last two games.'

In answer to the the question 'Why Furry Boots City?', the following explanation is from *The Scotsman* of 21 June 1995: 'Several, thousand that is, readers have asked why Aberdeen is sometimes referred to as furry boot city. The answer is a question: Furry boot y' frae?'

The term also reached the ears of Kamal Ahmed writing in *The Observer* of 20 July 1997 and I make no excuse for including this extract in full: 'Aberdeen is the only place I know where it snows on the beach. It's known as Furry Boots City, but this has nothing to do with the clothes people wear... The moniker refers to the greeting accorded strangers, "Furry boots ya fae?" Which means, "Whereabouts are you from?"'

The name seems to be here to stay, however, as the following from *The Scottish Express* of 24 September 2015 shows: 'In contrast, I may say, to all you belly-aching Borderer and fikes[1] from Furry Boots City.'

Pauline Cairns Speitel

---

[1] *fusspots*

GADGIE *noun* a boy, a man

The word gadgie is derived from Romany *gorgio* (a non-gypsy). In the DSL, gadgie, as recorded from the Gipsies of Kirk Yetholm c.1930, was any man who was not a gypsy. That this word was only in use by gypsies is further exemplified in the DSL by WB Watson in *The Roxburghshire Word-book*: 'Ay, ee're a shan[1] gadgee, no keepin yer tryst last night.' (1923).

However, this can be ante-dated to 1865 from *A History of the Gipsies: with Specimens of the Gipsy Language* by Walter Simson, whose father collected oral information from gypsies throughout Scotland. He attests the forms gaugie and gadgé, the latter also from Kirk Yetholm, to mean a man.

In the 20th century, the word was originally thought only to be used by children in the Edinburgh area but it has now passed into use by the general Scots-speaking population as shown in this example from Matthew Fitt: 'Twa mukkil gadgies wur camin owre, swellin oot thair chists an gein the young lad the evill,' in James Robertson's *A Tongue in yer Heid (*1994); and in the 21st century as shown by this example from *The Aberdeen Evening Express* of 6 March 2015: 'Maddeningly, a wayward finger has linked me up with a gadgie I knew in 19-oatcake whose life seems to have taken a bizarre turn.'

Finally, sometimes it can be shortened to gadge as used by Irvine Welsh: 'See that big skinny gadge wi the tarten skerf?' in *New Writing Scotland 11: The Ghost of Liberace* (1993).

Pauline Cairns Speitel

---

[1] *bad*

GLAIKIT *adjective* stupid, foolish

Scots have an amazing capacity for insulting each other. Glaikit seems to be one of our oldest terms for describing someone who is not intellectually blessed.

It makes its first appearance in the DSL with someone talking about the Scots as 'yon glakyt Scottis can ws nocht wndyrstand. Fulys[1] thai ar' in Henry the Minstrel's (who is perhaps better known as Blind Harry) *Acts and deidis of Schir William Wallace* (c.1478).

In the modern period, the DSL tells us that in addition to its original meaning it included '…thoughtless, irresponsible, flighty, frivolous (generally applied to women).' This is shown in the following citation from Shetland in George Temple's *Britta* from 1886: 'A young girl was more trouble than assistance in a house, Lasses were glaikit and needed looking after.'

In the late 20th century and into the 21st, the more familiar meaning describing someone with a vacant expression comes into being as in this example from John Byrne's *Your Cheatin Heart* (1990): 'Big glaikit-luckin' sod, turnt up out the blue in a raincoat no' aw that dissimilar tae…' Irvine Welsh, too, in *Trainspotting* (1993) forcefully describes someone with: 'His glaikit, open-moothed expression inspired ma instant contempt.' It is also used currently in our newspapers as shown by the following from *The Sunday Herald* of March 8 2016: 'The girl with the glaikit expression is wearing quite a smart hat and might be a pupil from a private school wondering how she ended up with this band of people.'

The origin of the word is obscure but, according to the DSL, it is perhaps a derivative of 'glaik', a noun meaning 'A derogatory term for a silly, light-headed or thoughtless person, especially a girl or woman'.

Pauline Cairns Speitel

---

[1] *fools*

GOWAN *noun* a daisy

Nowadays, gowan refers to the common daisy of lawns and daisy-chains but the DSL tells us that gowan was formerly a general name for various wild flowers: either yellow, or white with yellow centres, as shown by this quotation from John Brand's *A Brief Description of Orkney...* (1701): 'We saw the pleasantest mixture of Gowans so commonly called or Daisies white and yellow on every side of the way growing very thick.' Gowan was usually prefixed by either 'yellow' – for example, for buttercups, celandines, dandelions and marsh marigolds, or 'white', such as the ox-eye daisy.

There are many compounds of gowan as names for various flowers, eg horse-gowan, which generally referred to the ox-eye daisy but was used for a range of other flowers as well; ewe-gowan (the common daisy); and lucken-gowan (globeflower), whose petals form a closed, compact head. This quote from Allan Ramsay's poem 'The Young Laird and Edinburgh Katy' (1744) makes it clear that lucken-gowans were different from 'dazies': 'We'll pou the Dazies on the Green, The lucken Gowans frae the Bog.'

In later examples, gowans unqualified by a colour seem to refer only to daisies with white petals. So, we find this: 'The gowans whiten Struie brae, The Chapel haughs are green', from Hugh Haliburton's *Ochil Idylls* (1891), and this from John Buchan's *Poems, Scots and English* (1917): 'And lambs as thick on ilka green As simmer gowans.' It is clear in both these examples that the flowers are white. A later quote (*Scots Magazine*, 1944) refers to 'bold yellow gowans' which perhaps shows that yellow daisies have to be described as such.

Phrases include 'not to care a gowan' (not to care in the least) and to 'have the gowan under one's feet', which means to be (safe) in the open.

Ann Ferguson

HAFFET *noun* the temple, the cheek

The word haffet is derived ultimately from Old English *healfheafod*, literally 'half-head', which became halfheid in Older Scots, and haffet by the 16th century. It refers to the side of the head, above and in front of the ear.

Many of the examples in the DSL refer to haffets being struck or punched; for example, the *Glasgow Burgh Records* of 1575 tell us that 'Johne Gilmour is fund in the wrang for... stryking of him on the haffet with his neifis'.[1] Even worse, we learn from the *Register of the Privy Council of Scotland* of 1629, of an unfortunate victim who was subjected to 'A cruell straike..., whairwith he cutted away his lug with ane great part of his haffet.'

Moving away from violence, the poem 'In prais of his Maistres' from *The Poems of Alexander Montgomerie* (c.1605) tells us about some of the charms of the mistress in question: 'Hir curling loks, lyk golden rings, About hir hevinly haffats hings.' And still on a hairy theme, haffet-locks or simply haffets could refer to hair growing from or over the temples, as in Allan Ramsay's collection of poems *The Gentle Shepherd* (1725): 'Her Haffet-Locks hang waving on her Cheek', and in Burns' *The Cotter's Saturday Night* (1786): 'His bonnet rev'rently is laid aside, His lyart[2] haffets wearing thin and bare.'

From this it is easy to see how the current usage of haffit (now the more usual spelling) refers in joinery to the vertical sides of such things as bookshelves, cupboards, steps, church pews and dormer windows. This is illustrated in Neil Munro's *John Splendid* (1898): 'The love that set Provost Brown with his chair haffit close against his wife's, so that less noticeably he might take her hand in his below the table.'

Ann Ferguson

---

[1] *fists*
[2] *streaked with white*

HAGGIS *noun* a dish of oatmeal and offal

Haggis is defined in the DSL as 'A dish consisting of the pluck or heart, lungs and liver of a sheep minced and mixed with suet, oatmeal, onion and seasoning and boiled in a sheep's maw or stomach.' A more mouth-watering description comes from Dougal Graham's *Collected Writings* (1779): 'A piping het haggies, made of the creish[1] of the black boul horn'd Ewe, boil'd in the meikle bag, mixt with bear meal[2], onions, spice and mint.'

According to a dictionary informant from Kirkcudbright (1956), 'There was also a white or sweet haggis, of suet, oatmeal, currants, etc., cooked and sliced when cold and hard.' Fergusson, Burns' 'elder brother in the Muse', seems to have favoured the more familiar variety, 'a haggis fat, Weel tottl'd in a seything pat, Wi' spice and ingans weel ca'd thro'', the kind made famous around the world through the celebrated *Address to the Haggis* (1786) by Burns himself.

James Kelly's *Collection of Proverbs* (1721) declares 'A Man may love a Haggish that wo'd not have the Bag bladed in his Teeth' which means that a man may say or do something that he would not like to have cast up to him again later. It seems odd that visible dental evidence of having consumed our national dish should be perceived as shameful, but the word haggis itself is used as a term of disparagement when applied to a person. A haggis sale was the second day's auction at a large sheep sale when the stock might be expected to be of inferior or mixed quality. On the other hand, one usage in the DSL deserves wider currency. When you are looking for that tasteful expletive, you will find one in *The Disruption* by William Cross (1846): '"Principles! haggis bags!" exclaimed the lady.'

Chris Robinson

---

[1] *grease*

[2] *a type of barley*

HANTLE *noun, adverb* a large number or quantity

The origin of hantle is uncertain but it may be a reduced version of handful. However, whereas the modern usage of 'handful' implies a few, hantle refers to many, perhaps equivalent to 'quite a few' or 'a good few.' The earlier examples in the DSL show it in a plural context, as in 'A great hantle of bonnie braw well fac'd young lasses' from Jacob Curate's *The Scotch Presbyterian Eloquence displayed…* (1692), or 'a hantla stories O' blood, and dirt, and ancient glories' from Allan Ramsay's *Poems* (1876).

In the latter quote, the word 'of' has been reduced to an 'a' at the end of hantle, and often it is completely absent. Examples include this from John Learmont's *Poems* (1791): 'Thae, an' a hantle scenes that I cou'd name, Sal ay mak mine to me a happy hame' and this from Sir Walter Scott's *The Black Dwarf* (1816): 'They believed a hantle queer things in thae days, that naebody heeds since the lang sheep cam in.'

Hantle can also be used on its own to indicate an unspecified number of people, eg 'A hantel speak o' my drinking, but few ken o' my drouth' from John White's *Jottings in Prose and Verse* (1879). This meaning is often used by travellers, as in: 'The hantel aa celebrated with the laddie's nesmore,[1] who wis completely overjoyed' from Stanley Robertson's *Fish-Hooses* (1992).

Hantle can also be an adverb, often before a comparative. Thus we find 'It's a hantle caulder here than in London' from JM Barrie's *A Window in Thrums* (1889) and, from Andrew J Armstrong's *Friend and Foe* (1885), the rather understated: 'But to be strung up by the neck for the thing ye never did is a hantle waur[2] than the maist o' folk wad care to thole.'

Ann Ferguson

---

[1] *mother*
[2] *worse*

HAUGH *noun* a piece of level ground

Haugh, sometimes spelt hauch, also appears in Older Scots as halch. It usually rhymes with loch, but in some dialects the final consonant may disappear. It is a piece of level ground, generally alluvial river-meadow land. It comes from Old English *halh*, meaning a corner or nook. That 'l' has been lost, first from the pronunciation and then from the spelling, over the course of time. We find early Scottish written evidence of the word in place-names incorporated into Latin charters from around 1200.

Many of the quotations in the DSL suggest that haughs were fertile. William Nimmo's *A General History of Stirlingshire* (1817) tells us: 'The gravel and sand which is spread upon the clay, forms what are called our haughen grounds, that are most esteemed for corn and pasture.' The *Statistical Accounts for Lanarkshire* (1795) describes one agricultural practice: 'The haugh-ground is generally ploughed three and sometimes four years, for oats, and then allowed to lie as long in natural grass.' Other quotations suggest crops of peas or even daisies, but the river at the heart of the haugh could bring worse things than rich alluvial silt. The *Chronicles of the Atholl and Tullibardine Families* (1703) relate how 'There came a fearfull speat Wednesday last, which covered the greater part of the haugh of Tullichmulin with sand and stones.'

Allan Massie in the *The Last Peacock* (1980) describes another climatic drawback of such terrain: 'cold mist rose heart-high in the haughland' but, for all that, Violet Jacob maintains in *Songs of Angus* (1915) 'an auld man aye thinks lang O' the haughs he played amang'. On the whole, haughs are places of well-being and prosperity, and hence, when someone suffers a downturn in their fortunes, they are said 'to gang frae the hauch to the heather'.

Chris Robinson

HOGMANAY *noun* New Year's Eve

The earliest examples of Hogmanay relate not to the day itself but to a word shouted out on New Year's Eve to solicit a New Year gift. This gift usually consisted of food such as oatcakes, bread, fruit or the like, and was traditionally given to children on the last day of the year. The following 1692 quotation from the DSL explains this: '"It is ordinary among some plebeians in the South of Scotland to go about from door to door upon New-years Eve, crying Hagmane" from *The Scotch Presbyterian Eloquence Displayed* by Jacob Curate.'

From there, the meaning widened to refer to the gifts themselves, and both the call and the expected gift are indicated by the word in this 1842 quotation from Robert Chambers' *Popular Rhymes of Scotland*: 'The children on coming to the door, cry "Hogmanay!" which is in itself a sufficient announcement of their demands.'

Hogmanay came to mean any form of hospitality, especially a drink, given to a guest to celebrate the new year, or a gratuity given to tradespeople and employees. In James Nicol's *Poems* (1805), we read that 'The cotter weanies, glad an' gay… Sing at the doors for hogmanay' and, in a 1905 edition of the *Scottish Review*, 'The visitors never failed to receive their Hogmanay which consisted usually of bun, shortbread, and wine or whisky.'

Of course, the commonest meaning now is New Year's Eve itself, especially the evening. Sir Walter Scott in his *Journal* (ed. John Guthrie Tait) recorded that 'We… spent our Hogmanae pleasantly enough' (1830). To haud Hogmanay is to mark the passing of the old year by a convivial celebration, as in this from John Imlah's *May Flowers* (1827): 'Blithe, blithe we meet thegither, Here to haud our Hogmanae.' Some things don't change.

Ann Ferguson

JALOUSE *verb* to guess, suspect

This word seems to originate in the Old French verb *jalouser*, meaning to regard with jealousy, but the meaning is seen to have altered in Scots by the time of this quotation from the *Warrender Papers* (1586): 'Some amangis our selffis jaloux of your intelligence.' Some jalousins have a negative tone. For example, a Penninghame woman comes to the attention of the kirk, 'Being jealoused of uncleannes by reason of her and his staying both at home on the Lords day when others in the house went to Church', according the Session Book entry for 1700, but, as Nan Shepherd says in *Quarry Wood* (1928), 'jaloosin's nae provin'.

Often it simply carries a sense of surmise, as in this colourfully idiomatic remark from William Cross in *The Disruption* (1846): 'I jalouse they're a' o' ae hen's dab',[1] or a sense of realisation as in Robin Jenkins' *Leila* (1995): '"You've jaloused I'm staying the night," she whispered.'

The DSL includes Ulster Scots and this quotation from the *Belfast News Letter* (10 April 2004) clearly demonstrates the similarity of Ulster Scots to other dialects of the language, while pointing out one of the regional differences that enrich the leid: 'Frae quhat differ prittas ir cried ye're fit tae jalouse tha monie o' thaim wur bred athwort the sheugh i Scotlan.'[2] The works of John Galt are a very rich source of unusual Scots words and his *Ringan Gilhaize* (1823) provides us with a rare negative form of this word: 'We hae ta'en Robin Brown's cart frae him, that I might come wi 't unjealoused into the town.' If you come across 'unjaloused' anywhere else, please let us know.

Chris Robinson

---

[1] *hen's pecking ground*

[2] *From what the different potatoes are called you have to realise that many of them were bred across the Irish sea in Scotland.*

JOCK *noun* personal name

This name has become a generic term for a man. It is applied to farmworkers as in this example from the *Banffshire Advertiser* (1957): 'It wis a fairm jock ca'd Docken.' Robert Holman, among others, uses it of miners in *Character Studies* (1957): 'There was little thocht o' the hooses for the "coal jocks".'

In and beyond Scotland, soldiers in Scottish regiments are called Jocks and the dictionary preserves an instance of wartime relief for them, from the *St Andrews Citizen* (1940): '"Jock's Box", a fund organised for the purpose of sending comforts to Scottish troops.' Many of the examples in the dictionary suggest that Jocks tend to be ordinary working men, so much so that James Kelly in his collection of *Proverbs* (1721) cites the expression 'He's but Jock the Laird's Brother', and explains: 'The Scottish Lairds Concern and Zeal for the Standing and Continuance of their Families, makes the Provision for their younger Sons very small.' Hence, in Marion and Margaret Corbett's *Tales and Legends* (1828), we read: 'Mr Thomas is but Jock the Laird's brither, as a body may say, and hasna muckle gear.'

There are some Jocks, though, who have a claim to dictionary fame. One was the eponymous inventor of the 'Jock Scott, an artificial fly used by anglers, made from black and gold feathers with a hackle and invented by Jock Scott of Branxholm (1817–93), a keeper on Tweed', according to Francis Francis in *A Book on Angling* (1867).

Jock Wabster appears in contexts such as Sir Walter Scott's *The Antiquary* (1816): 'His mother fand it out, and then the deil gaed o'er Jock Wabster', signifying all Hell breaking loose, but what Mr Wabster did to deserve this is a mystery. Perhaps our best-known Jock is the one who brings together all Jocks and Jennies, lairds and their brothers, aa Jock Tamson's bairns.

Chris Robinson

LALDIE, GIE SOMETHING LALDIE *noun, phrase* to do something with enthusiasm

The DSL defines laldie as follows: 'A thrashing, a punishment, a drubbing, generally in phrases to get or gie laldie also figurative of any vigorous or energetic action.' Although the DSL sometimes uses rather quaint language – when was the last time we heard of someone getting a drubbing? – more or less all the senses of laldie are covered by the definition.

Punishment is neatly covered by the following from 1912 in a *Verse* by George Cunningham: 'Ye'll get laldy owre the bum.' Ouch. WD Cocker in his *Further Poems* of 1935 exemplifies a thrashing when describing Samson's encounter with the Philistines: 'He focht alane for Israel against the Philistine, An' fairly gied them laldie wi' the jaw-bane o a cuddie.'

Giving someone or something laldie is the most common phrase known to us today and used when describing something done enthusiastically or vigorously, but sometimes not necessarily well which is perhaps the implication given by Irvine Welsh in his short story from *Marabou Stork Nightmares* (1995): 'Ah mind ay ma Ma givin it laldy wi this yin. She sang it to me on my birthday.' William McIlvanney supplies a succinct figurative use in his 1983 novel *The Papers of Tony Veitch*: 'I'm on my way to the chiropodist's. Ma feet are givin' me laldy.'

Finally, in the 21st century, *The Herald* from 19 May 2000 supplies us with: 'William Bruce, a staunch Scottish nationalist, took his own piper with him to the Antarctic. There is a famous photograph of Piper Gilbert Kerr, giving it laldy.'

The origin, as with many of our words, is obscure. The DSL suggests it is perhaps a child's word but this implies no one, at the time they were compiling, really had any idea of its source.

Pauline Cairns Speitel

LET-DE-CAMP *noun* a camp bed

Just in case any hardy soul is planning a camping trip this summer, here is a useful, if rather obscure, word for a camp bed. Its chief interest lies in the amazing variety of guises in which it appears in Older Scots. The origin seems to be from French *lit-à-camp* or *lit-de-camp*, and this is compatible with such spellings as 'letacamp', 'littecamp' and 'letacamp'. The word also appears in Middle Dutch as *ledekant* and this may explain such Scots forms as 'lit(t)icant' and 'lit(t)igant.'

In case you are picturing a simple, folding affair of wood and canvas, various accounts indicate that even a temporary bed came with rich hangings. In the DSL, *The Register of the Great Seal of Scotland* (1545) records: 'Two letacampis ane of dames (damask) ane uthir of violet tafiteis frinyeit with gold'[1] at a cost of £140. At the other end of the market, a much less expensive one is bequeathed in an *Edinburgh Testament* of 1607: 'Ane liticall bed pryce l s.' They were not all that easy to transport. *The Accounts of the Treasurer of Scotland* (1538) describe the necessary accoutrements: 'Twa grete kow hidis to put the treis of the said littecamp in, the gidder witht twa lang furreons and twa cofferis to put the graith pertenyng to the said littecamp.' These were clearly not makeshift comfort for tents. We find them on ships and we also find them as an additional item in bedchambers as described in *The Sixth Report of the Historical Manuscripts Commission* (1562): 'An fixt bede of aik with ane litucampt of aik and ane stule.' James V seems to have been inordinately fond of them. We read in *Accounts of the Treasurer of Scotland* (1529), 'Deliverit for the Kingis grace thre letacampt beddis, ane in Striveling, ane in Edinburgh, the thrid in the wardrop of Edinburgh.'

Chris Robinson

---

[1] *Two letacampis, one of damask, another of violet taffeta fringed with gold.*

LORNE SAUSAGE *noun* square-shaped sausage meat

Lorne sausage, otherwise known as square sausage, sliced or slicing sausage is a traditional Scottish delicacy usually eaten at breakfast. Ex-pats pine for it in the same way they do for Scotland's national drink. It is made from uncased, uncooked, fresh beef sausage and cut in slices from a large block approximately 10cm square.

There have been many suggestions as to why it is called lorne sausage; one explanation given by Laura Mason and Catherine Brown in *Traditional Foods of Scotland* is: 'This became associated in Glasgow with the comedian Tommy Lorne, a popular music-hall performer for the decades between the world wars who often made rude jokes about the Glasgow square sausage describing them as "doormats".' (1999). This explanation is also given by *The Herald*: 'Many Scots, especially in the west, eschew link sausages for the square variety. Lorne sausage was named after Glasgow comedian Tommy Lorne who joked that Glasgow square sausage was akin to a doormat.' (16 November 2002).

Our research, some of which is published in the DSL, shows that this type of sausage is not confined to the west but is known throughout the country from Orkney down to Roxburgh.

Wider research uncovers an advertisement in the *Arbroath Herald and Advertiser for the Montrose Burghs* from A Blair & Co (butcher) which shows: 'Lorne sausages 6d per lb.'[1] This dates from 13 February 1896 which makes it seem unlikely that the sausage was named after the comedian who was only born in December 1890. What seems a more likely explanation is that it is named after the district of Lorne which now lies in the Argyll and Bute council area.

Pauline Cairns Speitel

---

[1] *sixpence per pound*

LUNCART *noun* a temporary shelter

Derived from Gaelic and originally referring to a harbour, encampment or fortified enclosure, a luncart was a temporary construction in a deer forest, or hunting lodge. This is clearly illustrated by the following 1632 quotation from the *Records of Invercauld* (1547–1828), edited by John Grant Michie: 'to big[1] and put up our lounkartis for the hunting. Over a century later we find Their huntings resembled campaigns; they lived in temporary cottages, called Lonquhards' from Thomas Pennant's *A Tour in Scotland* (1769).

Later, it could also be used for an open-air fireplace made of sods, with an iron bar across the top from which to hang a pot. In common with the hunting-related meaning, this was a temporary structure for a specific purpose; it could be used for cooking or washing, as in this description from *Scottish Notes and Queries* (1901): 'In high blanket washings at spring cleanings when a fire was kindled outside at a place called a luncart, near a burn or well.'

Moving away from the temporary nature of a luncart to its construction and shape, it could also be a hole made in a wall with a stone placed over it as a lintel, to create a gap for sheep to pass through or a burn to flow under. Thus, we find 'Lunkie, a hole in a dyke for the passage of sheep, filled up with thorns when inconvenient' from the *Transactions and Journal of the Dumfries and Galloway Natural History and Antiquarian Society* (1894).

Finally, from the notion of a gap in a long surface, luncart is used of a mass of one mineral within the layers of another. This use is illustrated by the following quote from *The Economic Geology of the Central Coalfield* (1917): 'This coal is overlain by... blackband ironstone, occasionally rising to 18 in "lunkers".'

Ann Ferguson

---

[1] *build*

MAR *verb* to harm, kill, maim

This word from the DSL is defined as 'to do bodily harm to, to strike at, maim, injure, kill; to defeat or punish' and the DSL gives the etymology as gypsy and is probably from Hindustani *marná* (to die), or Sanskrit *mārayate* (he kills). The word is recorded in the *Roxburghshire Wordbook* of 1923 by George Watson. Watson collected many words from the Kirk Yetholm gypsies.

However, the OED tells a different etymological story and gives various definitions among which are the following: 'To hamper, hinder, interfere with, interrupt, or stop (a person, event, etc). Now *Scots.*' and 'Originally: to do fatal or destructive bodily harm to (a person, limb, etc). Later also: to mangle, disfigure, or scar.' The OED gives a very full and thorough etymology tracing it back through Frisian and Old High German and encapsulating this in the succinct one line: 'A word inherited from Germanic.'

In an upcoming publication by SLD on the language of Scottish gypsies, the word is well-documented but as with many gypsy/Scots words that are shared, the gypsy version differs slightly so we still have 'to kill; to hurt or punish': *Mar the gaugie wi a clemmie, clach, or bar.*[1] but then there is another meaning 'to fight' as in the following example from *The Tin-Kin* by Eleanor Thom (2010): 'We don't get hit at home. Granny says the men can pummel their fists and mar with each other all they like…'

Neither of the above solves the etymological problem. Both are credible but I think in this case I would err on the side of the OED on the grounds that many words used by the travellers or gypsies were shared with the Scots. In earlier times, the gypsies avoided direct contact with the settled population but in the late 19th and 20th century, many travellers worked alongside house-dwellers, for example at harvest time.

Pauline Cairns Speitel

---

[1] *knock the man out with a stone*

MINCE *noun* nonsense, rubbish

Apart from haggis, mince and tatties is one of Scotland's most iconic national dishes which has nurtured many generations of Scots. Mince is so embedded in the national psyche that it has developed many unusual and inexplicable meanings.

It features in insults such as: 'He talks a lot o mince' (Michael Munro, *The Original Patter*, 1985) or if 'yer heid's fu o mince', you're either very confused or a complete fool, as illustrated by this example from *The Observer*: '...if tensions move the pace on to straight urban demotic, our respected Minister [David Blunkett] can expect to be told his heid's full of mince, or called, most woundingly, a numpty.' (10 August 1997) and, staying with politics, the *Daily Record* of 23 April 2015 tells voters that 'Only you can decide who's talking mince.'

Brian Montieth writing in *The Scotsman* notes: 'Nobody in England would use the word "mince" in this pejorative manner – while in Scotland it is common in colloquial parlance to say: "Your heid's full of mince", or "That's just mince" as a way of providing a semi-humorous put-down without resorting to swearing.' (22 April 2013).

A stupid person or persons can be described as being as 'thick as mince', as Hardeep Singh Kohli writes: 'Today's Tories, for all their privilege and erudite education, are arguably the least able coterie of Conservatives we have ever had in power. Basically, they are thick as mince.' (*The Sunday Herald*, 6 December 2015)

Finally, if someone is listless, idle or untidy, they are accused of being like a pound of mince: '... this frequenting of the Empress every afternoon and sitting about the house like a pound o mince isnae helping anybody.' (*The Independent on Sunday*, 26 June 2011) And an Edinburgh informant from 2005 tells an untidy person: 'Yer claes are hingin like a pun o mince.'

Pauline Cairns Speitel

NUMPTY *noun* a foolish person

Numpty was included in the 2005 supplement to the DSL with the following definition: 'a stupid person, an idiot'. In the revised edition of the *Concise Scots Dictionary*, the definition has been shortened to the kinder: 'a foolish person'.

Numpty is such a useful word that it has been adopted by the rest of Britain and has its own entry in the OED where it's given the label 'British slang, originally Scots'. Our first example in the DSL comes from *The Scotsman* of 7 January 1989: '…despite the MacDiarmid-led backlash of 60 years ago against Scottish kailyard numpties'.

A later example also from *The Scotsman* expands the meaning as in: 'The numpties remain. Some are so sunk in numptitude that only advanced genetic engineering, and the substitution of chimpanzee cranial parts, could effect a transformation towards more sentient life.' (27 March 2003) Numptitude was thought, by the editors of the 2005 supplement and of the revised *Concise Scots Dictionary*, to be a one-off coinage. No, it isn't – as the following examples recently added to our collected research shows. This is from *The Herald* of 7 August 2007: 'And Scottish Labour suffers from the Perverse Law of Numptitude which rules that those most vulnerable to losing their seats tend also to be the ones the party can least afford to lose.'

So numptitude has caught on and is still very much with us as we see from this example from the *Daily Star* of 8 November 2017: 'Lord Sugar wants the two rival outfits – Team Numptitude and Team Where The Hell Do The Producers Find These People…' Yes, lexicographers need to be very vigilant.

Pauline Cairns Speitel

ONDING *noun* a heavy fall of rain or snow

A heavy, continuous fall of rain or snow can be described as an onding. Formed from 'on-' in its adverbial sense of 'motion towards' and the verb 'ding' from Old Norse *dengja* meaning to beat, strike or batter, this is a word for all seasons. The prefixed noun appears in the late 18th century, but precipitation was dingin doun long before then. In Sir David Lindsay's *The Monarche* (c.1552), 'Frome the heuin the rane doun dang.'

There are few days when this quotation from Charles Keith's *The Farmer's Ha'* (1774) cannot be reprised: 'Rain we'll hae, Or on-ding o' some kind at least.' If we have to choose between ondings, Sir Walter Scott's in *Heart of Midlothian* (1818) comes firmly down on the side of snow: '"Look out, Jock; what kind o night is't?" "On-ding o snaw, father."'

Figuratively, the original sense of 'ding' as an onslaught reappears, usually in a dowie way. SR Crockett in *The Raiders* (1893) writes of 'The on-ding of their ill tongues' and, in TW Paterson's *The Wyse-Sayin's o' Solomon* (1916), we read that: 'The anger o' a king is like the on-ding o' daith itsel.' More chilling than either is the application of the word to a sermon in Jacob Ruddiman's *Tales and Sketches* (1828): 'The cauld glaff[1] of that ondinging [sic] has not left my inward parts to this blessed hour.'

Ondings can, however, be pleasurable. In John G Horne's *A Lan'wart Loon* (1928), 'At streek o' day, ae canty Spring, Tam wauken'd to the birds' onding.' Still looking on the bright side, it is worth remembering 'Life canna aye be yae[2] onding o' snaw' as Gilbert Rae remarks in *'Tween Clyde and Tweed* (1919). No indeed.

Chris Robinson

---

[1] *a sudden blast of cold air*
[2] *one, single*

PAGGER *noun, verb* fight

One area of language that is very scantily covered in the DSL is the language of Scottish gypsies and travellers which has passed into mainstream Scots usage. This was largely due to the paucity of information from these groups during the compilation of the DSL. With the recent revision of the *Concise Scots Dictionary*, the editors have tried to address at least some of these omissions.

The precise date when 'pagger' meaning 'a fight' or 'to fight' passed into general usage is unclear but it seems to be strongly connected to the Edinburgh area. It is possibly derived from Romany *poggra* (to break) or *pagard* meaning 'breathless.' Heinrich Moritz Gottlieb Grellmann in his 1787 *Dissertation on the Gipsies* collected the form *Pàkjum* (to break) from continental gypsies which is possibly the same word.

It is still very much in current usage as illustrated by the following example from the *Daily Record* of 2 March 2015 which is discussing the drinking habits of a minority of Hibernian football fans: 'The reality is that the drink has nothing to do with whether people want a pagger, it's the mentality of a small number of fans before they even have a tipple in the first place.' The verb is neatly illustrated by Robert McNeil when he writes about the ten plagues of Egypt and the flight of the Israelites in *The Scotsman* of 2 February 2006: 'The Israelites had actually been armed, and it's possible they turned round to pagger the charioteers, though you'd have thought Exodus would have made the most of this, instead of depicting Moses' mob as a bunch of saps saved by a dividing sea.'

In the current research of SLD, the earliest example comes from traveller author Betsy Whyte in her autobiographical *The Yellow on the Broom*, first published in 1979: 'She had been told that he was being held on suspicion of having given Johnnie Whyte a paggering. Johnnie was lying in Perth Infirmary unconscious, not expected to live.'

Pauline Cairns Speitel

PARTAN *noun* a crab

Borrowed from Gaelic and recorded in Scots texts from the 15th century, the partan has got its claws well and truly into the Scots idiom.

Early usages seem to mean any kind of crab but, later, partan usually denotes the edible crab. In the *Foulis Account Book* of 1700, we find that a luxurious dinner of 'lapster and partans and brandie' cost £2.18.6 but, less extravagantly, W Alexander in his 1871 novel *Johnny Gibb* writes of 'bawbee partans'. A halfpenny would have been all that a 'partan-fisted' or miserly person would have willingly paid.

The term partan-back was used in times past to refer to a soldier or redcoat, because of the colour of the cooked crab. A partan-taed person walks with in-turned toes. A partan-faced individual is not a pretty sight and if you really dislike someone you could call them 'a partan-faced sculduddery loon', a colourful phrase from J Carruthers' *A Man Beset* (1927). 'Fu as a partan' means full to the brim as in a vivid quotation from J Stewart's *Sketches* (1857): 'He had primed his proboscis [with snuff] till it was as "fou as a partin", and it is easy imagine the little man, as full as a partan of buttoned, brushed, and powdered pride' described by H Farnie in *Fife Coast* (1860).

Even when its insides are picked clean, the partan has its uses. Small children made partan-cairties, pulling the shells along on a string and the claw could be used as a pipe in which dried leaves of coltsfoot or 'shellaggie' (Latin: *tussilago*) was smoked as a substitute for tobacco. Gaining renewed popularity with gardeners is the partan-hoe, a cultivator with curved claw-like prongs. *The Press and Journal* of 21 April 1953 tells of the availability of 'Round Shovels, Dung Graips; Dutch, Draw and Parton Hoes'.

Chris Robinson

PAWKIE *noun, adjective* a fingerless glove, a mitten

A pawkie is defined in the DSL as 'A glove or mitten having one compartment only for all the fingers and one for the thumb' and, as a child, I had pawkies strung on a thread through my coat so that they would not be lost. The first instance of the word is from Lanark in 1822. In 2001, in the Borders, pawkies are recorded as 'mittens' in a *Glossary of Scots Words and Farming Terms*. The final example in the DSL comes from Edinburgh in 2003: 'In the winter pawkies keep yer hands warmer.'

It is not clear from the record if pawkie meaning everything from: 'Wily, sly, cunning, crafty' (first noted in 1782) or 'shrewd, astute, sagacious, "sharp", having one's wits about one, resourceful, "hard-headed"' (Ulster in 1929) are connected to the glove meaning at all.

The etymologies of both meanings are obscure. The DSL suggests that the gloves are from children's language while the OED suggests that the adjective is a derivative of 'pawk' with a 'y' suffix. The definition of 'pawk' is as follows: 'Scots. A trick, an artifice, a cunning device. Obsolete.' The OED originally said that the etymology was unknown but in their revised edition of September 2005 they suggest a Scandinavian source.

So, again, as with many Scots words we don't have any firm evidence. However, I personally think they are connected with one another but which came first? According to our evidence, it would seem to be the adjective.

Pauline Cairns Speitel

PECH *verb* to be out of breath, to pant

The DSL defines pech as 'To breathe quickly and in a laboured way, to pant with exertion', and it is in this last sense that it is most used today. An early example dates from the 16th century: 'He will tye the burthen of them on their owne backes whilest they grone and peach'[1] from Robert Rollock's *On the Passion*.

Moving forwards through the centuries, in 1754 we find 'At last, wi' great peching an' granin, we gat it up with a pingle'[2] from Robert Forbes' *A Journal from London to Portsmouth*; and a character in Sir Walter Scott's *The Bride of Lammermoor* (1819) declares: 'I hae been short-breathed ever since, and canna gang twenty yards without peghing like a miller's aiver.'[3]

A more modern example is from Ian Rankin's *Strip Jack* (1992): 'By the time he reached the second floor, he was peching and remembering exactly why he liked living in Patience's basement.' The fact that pech appears quite at home in a sentence that is otherwise in English is perhaps evidence that it is widely used.

By extension, to pech can also mean to go or work so as to pant or gasp with the exertion. The following 1949 quotation from the *Scots Magazine* illustrates this meaning and is another example of pech appearing in an otherwise English sentence: 'When we had peched at length to the top of the glen and stood on a vast heathery plateau, the light was going rapidly.'

As a noun, a pech is a laboured breath or gasp. John White in his *Jottings in Prose and Verse* (1879) refers to 'the old man's severe and continued pech-pech'. And predictably, the phrase 'oot o pech' means out of breath.

Ann Ferguson

---

[1] *He will tie the burden of them on their own back whilst they groan and pech.*
[2] *effort*
[3] *an old carthourse*

PIECE *noun* a bit, a portion; a sandwich or packed lunch

Many of the senses of piece are to do with food, particularly referring to small or portable portions. Early examples in the DSL illustrate the typically Scots usage without the word 'of', as in the *Glasgow Burgh Records* (1590): 'and byting of hir through the arme and Latting the peice flesche quhilk scho bait fall in the watter',[1] and in Samuel Colville's *The Whig's Supplication* (1681): 'There a piece beef, there a piece cheese lyes.'[2]

Specifically, a piece can be a sandwich or single slice of bread with butter, jam, cheese or the like on it, as in: 'I like a piece on cheese for my lunch' from Edinburgh (1994) or, in William McIlvanney's *Walking Wounded* (1989): 'Would ye like a piece on sausage?' These examples also show the Scots usage of 'on' in the context of pieces.

More generally, a piece can be any portable snack or packed lunch, which may or may not involve bread. For instance, William Bennet refers to a stone-dyker in *Traits of Scottish Life* (1830): 'During the day, he subsists on his piece.' This meaning has given rise to various piece-related compounds, such as piece-box, piece-bag, piece-poke, play-piece (for playtime at school) and piece time, as in 'I'll have that bridie at piece time.' (Highlands, 1960s)

A baby's piece or bairn's piece is a small portion of, for example, bread and cheese – or, more recently, christening cake, offered to the first person encountered after a christening. A bride's piece is a tea or light meal provided at a wedding by the bride's parents. Finally, the writer of this plea for pieces which appeared in the *Border Magazine* (1937) would be glad to hear that pieces are alive and well: 'All carried lunches were "pieces" then. I hope you have not begun to call them lunches.'

Ann Ferguson

---

[1] *...and biting her through the arm and letting the piece of flesh which she bit fall into the water.*
[2] *There's a piece with beef and there's a piece with cheese sediment.*

PLAID, PLAIDIE *noun* a rectangular length of twilled woollen cloth

The origin of plaid is uncertain. It is perhaps formed from 'ply' to fold or from Gaelic *plaide* (a blanket).

A plaid or plaidie is an oblong strip of cloth which is usually made of wool, frequently with a tartan pattern. Plaids or plaidies were originally worn in rural areas by outdoor agricultural workers such as shepherds.

The earliest example recorded in 1510 in the DSL comes from *Rentale Dunkeldense: being Accounts of the Bishopric* (1505–17): '[To dye 4 ells] lie plaidis [for my lord 2 s.]'[1]

Burns in his poem 'O' Wert Thou in the Cauld Blast' uses plaidie figuratively to mean a shelter: 'My plaidie to the angry airt, I'd shelter thee, I'd shelter thee.' Burns wrote this poem in 1796 from his deathbed for the young Jessie Lewars, a family friend who helped look after him in his final days. It is reported to be the last poem he wrote.

In more modern times, 'plaid' or 'plaidie' has been used to refer to a shawl or stole: 'Are you no too warm wi that plaidie roond ye?' (Oral example from Edinburgh, 2009)

Finally, plaids were not always made from wool. Sometimes more luxurious material was used as shown in this example from Anna Blair's 1990 novel *The Rowan on the Ridge*: 'There was no sudden windfall of wealth at the farm but it prospered a little more with each year's cycle and Susannah in time had a new silk plaid and two dresses as well as her working bodices and thibet[2] skirts.'

Pauline Cairns Speitel

---

[1] *To dye four lengths of cloth in a liquid dye for my lord. Cost two shillings.*
[2] *A kind of fine wool used in women's clothing.*

PURVEY *noun* the food supplied for a gathering

Scots is a living language. So, although words die out, new words are still being created. This week's word is not one that I knew until I moved to West Lothian. I heard it frequently there and it is a useful addition to my vocabulary. After all, the quality of the purvey is important to the success of any social gathering. It is used mainly of funerals but also of weddings and parties in general. It did not appear in the DSL until the supplement of 2005.

This supplement was the product of SLD's ongoing research. The first record of purvey in the record comes from an Angus speaker in 1990 who informed the dictionaries that purvey is a noun meaning a 'catering supply.' Such new information is stored until corroboration comes along and more examples start rolling in.

From *The Herald* (26 April 1996) we have: 'They explained that they were mourners and, having seen their granny off at the crematorium and having consumed the purvey, thought they would carry on the mourning at the karaoke on the grounds that the old gal would have liked that.' *The Herald* (10 October 2000) obliges with a further quotation: 'Perhaps the only bitter taste was when Labour Party organisers objected to the quality of the cups and saucers supplied by Glasgow Council for the purvey back at Kelvingrove.' Ian Pattison in *A Stranger Here Myself* (2001) refers to a traditional funeral 'ham purvey'. Clearly this new use of purvey comes from the long-established verb. We would be interested to know whether its use is spreading and, if so, into which areas. If you live outside the Central Belt and use this word or hear it used in your area, please let us know.

Chris Robinson

SCAFFIE *noun* a street sweeper, a refuse collector

The origin of 'scaffie' is given in the DSL as '...a diminutive of English scavenger' and is defined as 'a street sweeper'.

Scaffies first appear in the second half of the 19th century, presumably as a result of town councils taking control of street cleaning and the general cleanliness of the urban landscape. The first mention of them in the DSL is from Angus in William Blair's *Chronicles of Aberbrothock* (1853): 'Hecklers, an' wabsters, an' baxters, an' scaffies, an' wives, an' bairns, dowgs an' cats.'[1]

In the 20th century, the first example is a compound 'scaffy bucket' from the *Kelso Chronicle number 8* from 1918: 'She was too late for the scaffy bucket'; other compounds include 'scaffy cairt' from the *Buchan Observer* of 7 February 1967: 'Not up in the morning early enough to catch the scaffy cairt.' In Dundee David A MacMurchie recalls in his memoir *I Remember another Princes Street!* (1986): 'Once upon a time, all employees of the cleansing department except office staff were termed "scaffies".'

In the 21st century, we have a quote from the *Daily Mail* of 7 April 2003: 'On the pedestrian overpass, a startled scaffie has surrendered his broom.' And that scaffies are still around today is illustrated by the following from *The Herald* of 25 June 2014: 'My latest purchase from an online tax evader is a pair of 32-inch long and strong litter pickers. For these I paid the princely sum, including postage, of £10.73. Thus, for just over a fiver, I have acquired the wherewithal to become a bona fide scaffie.'

Scaffie has also extended its meaning to become an adjective meaning something shabby or disreputable: 'Fit's the deal with that [the chancellor's briefcase] onywye? It ayewis minds me on Paddington Bear. It's a gye scaffie looking thing, though, is it?' from *The Press and Journal* of 24 March 2014.

Pauline Cairns Speitel

---

[1] *Flax dressers, and weavers, and bakers...*

SCALDIE *noun* a non-traveller, a house dweller

In the language of the Scottish travellers, a scaldie is a person from the settled, house-dwelling population. The definition given for scaldie in the DSL is 'An unfledged young bird, a nestling' but the evidence for this meaning is sparse with only one citation from Ulster in S MacManus' *Land of the O'Friel's* published in 1903: 'I got... a linnet's nest with scaldies.' So the travellers' meaning of scaldie may be a development from this.

The settled population were viewed with wariness by the traveller community and, of course, the travellers were viewed likewise by non-travellers. An example from *The Yellow on the Broom* by Betsy Whyte writing in 1979 gives a flavour of this mutual suspicion when camping in the berry fields: 'We children and young people were given strict orders not to go near the tents of the scaldies (the lower-class town dwellers) as many of them were sure to be hotching with vermin or consumptive...' Betsy Whyte, however, did acknowledge that the scaldies had their own problems: 'If no money was coming into a house the scaldies suffered much more than we did, as few of them could turn their hand to anything that would bring in a few coppers.'

Jess Smith writing in 2012 in her history of the travelling peoples, *The Way of the Wanderers: The Story of Travellers in Scotland*, recalls when both travellers and scaldies made a living in the summer months also in the berry fields: 'During the Glasgow Fair Fortnight many came from there to make a few extra shillings at the berries, Perth scaldies (our name for non-tinker folk), caveys from Caithness (so-called because of folk-tales about the last of the Vikings hiding in caves at Caithness)...'

In the 21st century, I wonder how many of the now mostly settled traveller community would call non-travellers 'scaldies'.

Pauline Cairns Speitel

SCART *verb, noun* scratch, scrape

Scart has a long history. It usually refers to scratching with nails or claws, and there are various references in the DSL to people scarting their own faces. For example, in the 14th century *Legends of the Saints* (John Barbour, 1380) we read: 'With hyre handis [she] skartyt hir face', and in *Poems of John Stewart of Baldynneis* (c.1590): 'His hands outragius did his visage skart Maist horribile.'

As for scarting others, there is plenty of evidence for that too. In George Bannatyne's *Manuscript written in Tyme of Pest* (1568), there is the threat: 'I sall yow skart quhill that ye bleid.' and in Allan Ramsay's *A Collection of Scots Proverbs* (1776) the somewhat off-putting 'Biting and scarting is Scots fowk's wooing.' We hope not.

Scart could also be used of an animal scraping or scratching for food, as in 'Jenny's hens scartin' up his corn seed' from JL Waugh's *Robbie Doo* (1912).

Scarting features in various compounds and phrases. A scartin post is a scratching post for cattle and to scart a grey pow[1] is to be old, as in: 'There's ane o' the twasome will never scart a grey pow' from *The Notandums* (1890) by John Service. To scart someone's buttons referred to drawing one's fingers down another's jacket buttons, as a challenge to fight. This is illustrated in James Hogg's *Three Perils of Woman* (1823) where a character declares: '"I winna sit nae langer to be mockit. I scart your buttons, sir."'

A more figurative use of scart referred to scraping things together or scrimping. The latter is clearly illustrated in this quote from Sir William Mure's *True Crucufixe* (1629): 'If loue of money... Moue thee to scrape, to scart, to pinch, to spare...'

Ann Ferguson

---

[1] *head*

SCOMFISH *verb, noun* to stifle; to disgust or sicken

The definition of scomfish (pronounced scumfish) in the DSL is 'to suffocate, stifle, choke; to stop the breath from want of air, from smoke, heat, stench or the like' – so to be scomfished is altogether an experience to be avoided.

Among the more colourful examples are 'Gie up your house, now, mither deere, The reek it skomfishes me' from Francis *Child's English and Scottish Ballads* (1766); 'Feech! what a scuneris guff![1] Anouch tae skumfish me!' from WT Dennison's *The Orcadian Sketch-Book* (1880); and from Archibald Crawford's *Tales of my Grandmother* (1825), the somewhat tragic 'Jenny Gorlin, that scomficed her ain bairn, for fear o' the cutty stool.'[2]

Scomfish also came to mean to disgust or sicken in general, as in JM Barrie's *The Little Minister* (1891): 'It's fair scumfishing to hear her blawing about thae teeth.' And an Edinburgh source quoted their 'ancient granny' (born c.1850) describing a 'mechantoder[3] that wad scomfish a cuddy'. There is also the more figurative 'The tongue o her wad hae scomfish't a jaikdaw' from Helen Warwick's *Tales from 'The Toon'* (1914).

As a noun, scomfish could mean a suffocating atmosphere, a state of suffocation or fug. CM Costie in *Benjie's Bodle* (1956) says: 'He raised sic a scunface that you couldna' see the face o' the clock.' And from the sense 'to disgust' it could also refer to a strong dislike, a feeling of repulsion, which is how it is used in the phrase 'to tak a scumfish at', meaning to be disgusted at or take a strong dislike to. Scomfish is a shortened form of discomfit, originally with the more general meaning of a defeat in battle.

Ann Ferguson

---

[1] *Wow! What a terrible smell.*
[2] *The cutty-stool was a stool in a church where 'offenders against chastity' were forced to sit*
[3] *A bad odour*

SCOOBY *noun* a clue

Rhyming slang is sometimes thought to be strictly the domain of the Cockney but it has been utilised as a device by Scots speakers too.

Scooby Doo, the cartoon character created for the Hanna-Barbera Productions in 1969, is an addition in the second edition of the *Concise Scots Dictionary* because, as far as we can ascertain, in the early 1990s his name was used as the rhyming slang for 'clue'. Although I cannot find any examples of his name in full, it seems always to be shortened to 'Scooby' as in 'I haven't got a scooby'. The earliest example that we have in our research records comes from *The Herald* of 14 May 1993: 'Your lawyer telling youse that he husnae a scooby and youse can jist take a wee tirravie[1] tae yersel.' (which, incidentally, also appears in the revised OED from 2006).

The fact that the term is used in print in a national newspaper illustrates that it was in common enough use to be understood by the general public but as with many new Scots words finding evidence in print is very difficult.

Many of the current examples seem to be concerned with our national obsession with football as this example from Grant Stott writing in the *Edinburgh Evening News* of 24 January 2011: 'If I had a pound for every time someone has asked me or texted me the question, "Big man, what's happening with yer team?" I'd have?… well, a few quid now. And the answer is always the same. I haven't got a Scooby.'

There is as ever, as with much of research, a hunt on for earlier examples of this phrase.

Pauline Cairns Speitel

---

[1] *a fit of rage or bad temper*

SCUNNER *verb, noun* loathing, disgust, aversion

Among the examples in the DSL of the verb scunner (to engender disgust or loathing) is this from John Wilson's *Noctes Ambrosianae* (1826, in *Blackwood's Magazine*): 'Be you strong of stomach, and... dinna scunner.' It is often used with 'at', as in John Buchan's 1927 novel *Witch Wood*: 'There are times when I scunner at my native land.'

It also means to cause such feelings, as in this from *Blackwood's Magazine* (1820): 'The scunnering smell o' an acre o' corses',[1] or this from *The Quarry Wood* by Nan Shepherd (1928): 'The smell of his body scunnered them.'

More figuratively, to scunner is to make one disgusted, bored or or fed up. Thus in JM Barrie's *The Little Minister* (1891), a character declares: '"I was fair scunnered at Tammas the day"' and in George M Gordon's *The Auld Clay Biggin'* (1911), we read that 'He had hated the vera sicht o' weemen, as he said they fair scunner't him.'

As a noun, a rather precise meaning of scunner is explained in Margaret Oliphant's *The Ladies Lindores* (1883): 'A scunner is a sudden sickening and disgust with an object not necessarily disagreeable – a sort of fantastic prejudice, which there is no struggling against.' In Lennox Kerr's *Woman of Glenshiels* (1935), we read: 'It fair gies ye the scunner the way they all grumble' and in Robert J. Muir's *The Mystery of Muncraig* (1900), 'He had never told his weakness to his brother, having had a 'scunner' against doing so.'

In more recent times, we see derivatives such as scunnersome and scunneration. *The Herald*, in 1994, suggested that: 'Only the most introspective among us can contemplate our navels for any length of time without a degree of scunneration setting in.'

Ann Ferguson

---

[1] *corpses*

SCUTTER *verb* to botch, make mess. *noun* a mess, a shambles

The origin of scutter is obscure but the DSL suggests that it is an alteration of skitter... and perhaps also influenced by English scutter (to scurry).

It is a word very much associated with Aberdeen and the surrounding district of the North East of Scotland. It was first noted as being from this area in John Jamieson's 1825 supplement to his *Etymological Dictionary of the Scottish Language*.

The first written example we have comes from *Poems, chiefly in the Buchan Dialect* by William Scott, published in 1832 and describes spattering or splashing: 'Tak' aff their milk, an' leave their edders[1] teem[2]. An' trail the raip, an' scutter a' the reem.'[3]

Scutter also means to engage in time-wasting activities: 'Fat an awfu' scutterin' wauy o' daen' it is hae'n tae flit?' from *Bon-Accord* of 12 November 1887.

An example of the noun meaning something troublesome and irritating is illustrated by the following (not very politically correct) example from WHL Tester's *Poems* from 1870: 'Auld maiden ladies – a scunner an' scutter.'

People or animals who work in an ineffective, muddled or dirty manner are included in the following from the *Mearns Leader* of 22 February 1957: 'Tae treesch[4] wi' that sweet-mou'd scutter o' a beast finever she tak's a tigg[5] o' this kine.'

In more modern times we return to splashing in water. From *The Aberdeen Evening Express* of 11 June 2004: 'Saturday morning was a scorcher, so we grabbed our swimming cozzies, a picnic and headed for one of the tiny beaches round the loch, surrounded by thick trees. We scuttered about in the water then lay down on the sand.'

Pauline Cairns Speitel

---

[1] *udders*

[2] *empty*

[3] *cream*

[4] *cajole*

[5] *a sudden, whim, a huff*

SHAN *adjective* bad quality, inferior

The earliest meaning of shan in the DSL is 'Of poor quality, bad, mean, worn-out, shabby, pitiful, paltry' and the first example is from the poet Alan Ramsay in his *Poems* illustrates this: 'Shaws[1] but ill Will, and looks right shan...'

The second meaning in the DSL is 'bashful, timid, backward, chicken-hearted, frightened' as in the example from Douglas McKenzie writing in the magazine *Chapman Number 81* in 1990: 'Ma Shughy is a barry gadge, No shy, no shan, a total radge.'

Shan was originally a term used widely within the traveller community and has developed many meanings – a shan gadgie was a non-traveller man seeking a prostitute as illustrated by Betsy Whyte in her autobiographical *Yellow on the Broom* (1979): 'I hadn't wanted to desert her in case he was a "shan gadgie" – an unpleasant man looking for a woman.' The term was eventually borrowed by the settled community and is in current use by authors such as Irvine Welsh in his short story collection *Marabou Stork Nighmares* (1996): 'I fancied myself as a hard **** and it was f***** shan to have that for a brother.'

Other uses include 'shan shop' which is a term for a baker shop selling day-old bread, as exemplified by Jimmy Boyle's *A Sense of Freedom* (1977): 'On a Saturday morning Harry and I would get up and go down to the shan shop at the bottom of our street...' Shan was originally believed to be a word which was used exclusively by Travellers, whose origins were obscure, but later research revealed that it is in fact a loan word from Gaelic *seann* (old, aged, ancient or antique).

Pauline Cairns Speitel

---

[1] *shows*

SHILPIT *adjective* feeble

A *Dictionary of the Older Scottish Tongue* has little evidence of the early use of shilpit but what it has is splendid. It cites Sir Robert Moray's *Letters to Alexander Bruce, 2nd earl of Kincardine*, wherein shilpit is used of wine in the sense of insipid or lacking body: 'I think not you did amisse to abstain from wine a while... seing... the best you have is but shilpit stuff' (1658). It also gives a noun from shilpit used in the *Diary of Sir Archibald Johnston of Wariston* (1637): 'Lord, thou knouest... the schilpitnes of my wit.'

It is not until the 19th century that this word comes close to its modern popularity. At the start of that century, Sir Walter Scott is still using it of insipid wine in *Waverley* (1814): 'He pronounced the claret shilpit.' However, by that time it is also being used of peelie-wallie people or unhealthy features. So in *the Transactions of the Highland and Agricultural Society of Scotland* (1832) we have 'The white-faced shilpit-like wretches.' Ian Maclaren paints a clear picture in the *Young Barbarians* (1901): 'He was a little man, and gey shilpit about the neck' and we can hold out little hope of improvement for the character under discussion in John Tweeddale's *Moff* (1895): '"Hoo's 'e lookin'?" "He's shilpiter."'

R Crombie Saunders uses the word in a poetic context in *The New Makars* edited by Tom Hubbard (1991): 'The shilpit mune of autumn Keeks wanly thro the mirk', but it is mainly a word embedded in everyday speech and most of us now recognise the set phrase employed by George MacDonald Fraser in his hilarious account of army life, *The General Danced at Dawn* (1970): 'Baxter hesitated. "He called me a shilpit wee nyaff, sir." The president stirred. "He called you what?" Baxter coloured slightly. "A shilpit wee nyaff."'

Chris Robinson

SHUNKIE, SHUNKEY *noun* a WC

Until relatively recently I thought this was a word confined to Edinburghers but an oral example from 2008 shows me otherwise: 'A shunkey is an ootside lavvy at a fitba match – especially Pitoddrie.' Pitoddrie is well past the Edinburgh's boundaries. An outside convenience is probably referred to in this example from John Hamilton's 1900 *Rustic Rhymes and Revelry*: 'But we wouldn't put it past him, for Lachie must have been shut in the shunkie when the issue of brains were being allocated.'

The above was missed when the entry in the DSL was compiled and the original entry in the DSL is very sparse with only two citations from 1970 without examples. Most modern examples come from the 2005 supplement to the DSL with more information coming from SLD's current research into the word.

The following is from the 2005 supplement: 'Then, half an hour after that, when Big Isa wanted to go to the shunky, I found him there wi' his troosers round his ankles.' This example from Fred Urquhart in *Chapman Magazine* from 1986 seems to indicate that this encounter took place in a shared toiled in a tenement.

Examples from our current research include this one from Kenny Farquarson writing in *Scotland on Sunday* on 8 August 1993: 'Irvine Welsh, in the kitchen of his second-floor flat overlooking Leith Links, offers a can of export and talks about a friend of his who tentatively suggested including a glossary so that posh people could understand words like barry, radge, swedgin, shan, biscuitersed, skaggybawed, shunky, spawny and donks. "No way," he says.'

Finally, in 2017, Keith Aitken writing in *The Scottish Express* of 11 May 2017 observes: 'A couple of years back, a public shunkey near us was closed in order to curb the fiscal deficit. Now plans are afoot to turn it into... a bank.'

The etymology is obscure.

Pauline Cairns Speitel

SKELF *noun* a splinter

The Scots have many different words for splinters. The DSL records many and a number of them begin with 's' as in: spail, sheave, sclinder, skink and skelb, plus many more. There are, however, exceptions such as cootle and flog.

Skelf is one of the more versatile 'splinters' as in the following example from the memoirs of his own life by Sir James Melville from around 1610: 'The King Hendre II being hurt in the head with the skelv of a spair… at the triumphall justin[1] of his dochters mariage.' It seems that the wedding celebrations of our ancestors could result in more than just a hangover.

Our more modern meaning of skelf being a small fragment of wood embedded in the skin makes a comparatively late appearance in the DSL and is from a 1947 radio programme, perhaps recalled by some readers, called the McFlannels written by HW Pryde: 'He had a skelf in his finger.' Of course, people are still getting skelfs (never skelves) as shown in the following late 20th century example from Christopher Brookmyre's *Quite Ugly One Morning* published in 1996: '…and as its exposed floorboards were not of the trendy polished variety, he figured he would be picking skelfs out of his bare feet all afternoon.'

A skelf can also be a small insignificant or very thin person as illustrated by Chris Dolan in his *Poor Angels* from 1995: 'As if any respectable American employer would have taken on a wee skelf of a lassie with no qualifications to her name…' which implies that the poor lassie was both insignificant and skinny.

The origin is probably from Dutch *schelf* (a flake or scale).

Pauline Cairns Speitel

---

[1] *jousting*

SKITE *verb* to dart, shoot through the air, fall or be driven in a slanting direction

Skite is one of these Scots words that defies translation into English. We find it used of the unimpeded slanting motion of a shooting star in a poem by Allan Ramsay (1720): 'Like a shot Starn, that thro' the Air Skyts East or West with unko Glare.' Equally, it can refer to something rebounding or glancing off course. Hail, for example is often described as skiting and this usage is reflected in a simile by J Tweeddale in *Moff* (1895): 'It only skited off 'im like a shoor o' hailstanes.' A particularly vivid example comes from the *Buchan Observer* (28 Aug 1951): 'Frost so keen as to make the scythe blades 'skyte', when they came in contact with the flattened and whitened corn.'

If someone skites on ice, it is a much more dramatic mishap than just slipping. Skiting can be unpredictable. Robin Jenkins illustrated the unpredictability of skiting in *The Thistle and the Grail* (1954): 'Don't tell me he's bald, for I don't trust centre-forwards wi' slippery heids, though, mind you, the goalie can never be sure what way the ball's going to skite.' It also implies speed as in this item from *Peeblesshire News* (28 October 1960): 'He skites through the racin' page like a rid hot knife through a quarter o' margarine.'

Literal or figurative violence may also be also involved as in Joe Corrie's *The Last Day* (1928): 'Idle time an' wee peys¹ sune skite the beauty aff us.'

As a noun, it can mean a glancing blow, a piece of mischief, a squirt of liquid, a short sharp shower or a small quantity of drink. 'On the skite' denotes a bit of a spree and in the *Anthology of Orkney Verse* edited by EW Marwick (1949), we cheerfully read that, 'Vikings on the skite find Valhalla for wan night.'

Chris Robinson

---

¹ *pays ie wages*

SLAISTER *noun* a messy person. *verb* to make mess or work in a sloppy fashion

We Scots, it would seem, are very messy people. We appear to have more than our share of words for messes and causes of mess.

The OED gives the origin of slaister as 'obscure' and the DSL says that its immediate origin is uncertain but it ultimately may have its roots in Scandinavia.

Slaisters are not confined to any one dialect area of Scotland but they range from Orkney, this example from 1950: 'What a slester yir makin' o' dain' that' to this 21st century example from *The Herald*: 'For while Keep Scotland Beautiful's ambition is laudable, it knows better than most that when it comes to tidying up we are a nation of slaisters.' Yes, quite. Possibly not a national characteristic we should be proud of!

The Edinburgh poet JK Annand, who wrote mainly for children, paints a picture of what one hopes is children playing in puddles: 'Seekin worms, seekin grubs, Slaisterin in the clarty dubs.' (*Sing it Aince*, 1965)

Our earliest example of a person being a slaister with food or drink is from Roxburgh (1825) in John Jamieson's *Etymological Dictionary of The Scottish Language*, first published in 1808. In *The Scotsman* of 26 July 1954 we have: 'He maladroitly spilled his tea on the glistening tablecloth, and was promptly but not unkindly called a wee slaister.'

Another early example also relates to eating or drinking messily and comes from Robert Chambers' *Traditions of Edinburgh*, published in 1825: 'A wheen puir slaister-kytes.'[1]

Finally, this theme continues into the 21st century with this example from *The Scotsman* of 14 December 2001: 'But appearances can be deceptive, and Kiernan is soon picking the raisins out of the BBC Scotland scones and spilling his coffee everywhere – he's a right slaister.'

Pauline Cairns Speitel

___

[1] *messy stomachs*

SMIT *noun* a spot, blemish; *verb* to stain, infect

At an early period, we find this word in a figurative context. John Barbour's *Legends of the Saints* (1380) has the following examples: 'Criste hym chesit fore to be But smyt of flesche in chastite[1] and The feynd… thocht that he wald put a smyt In hyr gud nam, for to fyle it.'[2]

Another early sense, illustrated in the DSL, is to put an identification mark on a sheep. Hence, 'You must have the tarr pigg[3] by your belt, and be ready to give a smott to every one of Christ's sheep' is the instruction given by John Livingstone (1660) in William Tweedie's *Select Biographies*. Returning to *Legends of the Saints*, we find the sense more familiar to modern Scots speakers: 'his seknes smytit hym sare.'

Moving into the 20th century, this threat is from Andrew Wilson's *Till'Bus Comes* (1934): 'If I had measles I'd sit on your doorstep till I gied ye the smit!' Allan Ramsay's *Collection of Scots Proverbs* (1736) gives a variant of the English proverb regarding one rotten apple: 'Ae scabbed sheep will smit the hale hirdsell.'[4]

'Smittle' is a way of saying 'highly infectious' and WD Cocker in his *Further Poems* (1935) rewords Ramsay's proverb: 'A smittle thing the mawk,[5] Yae flee contaminates a flock.' 'Smittin' is another possibility, as in James Brown's *The Round Table Club* (1873) where we find the question: '"Is't smittin', like sma' pox?"' A sad declaration comes from JM Barrie's *The Little Minister* (1891): 'He said "I'm smitted" and went home to die' but not all smits are bad. Robert Ford tells us in *Tayside Songs* (1895): 'A sleekie, weel-penn'd billet-doux, Wi' love's burnin' ardour, wad smit them' but, if love's ardour is unwelcome, there is no need to despair for, according to P Buchan's *Mount Pleasant* (1961), 'There's cures for ills that smit the hert.'

Chris Robinson

---

[1] *Christ chose him for to be smitten of flesh in chastity.*

[2] *The feind… thought that he would put a smit in her good name, to foul it.*

[3] *pot*

[4] *One infected sheep will smit the whole flock.*

[5] *maggot*

SNED *verb* to cut, prune, lop

Snædan in Old English referred predominantly to lopping trees and it is no surprise to find it used similarly in Older Scots. John Knox writes in the *History of the Reformation in Scotland* (1547), 'Otheris sned the branches of the Papistrie, but he stryckis at the roote.' The ancient meaning has survived. *The Scotsman* (1998) describes the wartime employment of women in forestry: '…they undertook the work, proving they were as hardy as men. Training camps were set up to teach the women how to hold an axe, lay-in, fell, sned and cross-cut the timber.' Ulster Scots provides another modern example in the *Belfast News Letter* (2003): 'Wi holly tae sned an puddins tae boil Ahm badly fashed fer hits tha near Christmas. Dis onieboadie ken tha Ulster Scots fer "Bah Humbug"?'

Other plants come in for snedding. Michael Traynor's *The English dialect of Donegal* (1953) gives an example: 'Snedding turnips in winter is many a time sair work' and Jamieson's *Etymological Dictionary of the Scottish Language* (1825) defines sned-kail as 'colworts or cabbages, the old stalks of which, after they have begun to sprout, are cut off and left in the ground for future product. The cutting is supposed to prevent their going to seed.' There is exuberant snedding by Burns in *To a Haggis* (1786): 'Legs an' arms, an' heads will sned Like taps o' thrissle.'

However, in Shetland, sned describes a sheep-mark with a piece cut aslant from the top of the ear. This very regional use probably comes from Old Norse *sneitha* (to cut), which survives in Faroese, where it shares the Shetland dialect sense. In the OED, the Old Norse descendant appears as *snathe*, amazingly with the same limited sense as Old English *snædan* and our own Scots sned – to lop trees. Languages get into some right fankles.

Chris Robinson

SNOTTUM *noun* a long iron pole with a hook at one end

This word comes from the Romany and the travelling peoples of Scotland and its origins are completely obscure. A snottum has many uses but it was mainly used to hang a pot or kettle over an outdoor fire. Other uses include that it was used as a bore for tent pegs or as a fairly stout and formidable weapon.

It has not yet been added to the DSL and there is no trace of it in the OED.

It seems to only be in use among Scottish travellers and gypsies. The Romany word for iron is *saster* or *sauster*, and the word for copper is *sonnasaster* which seems to be a compound made up from *sonnakey*, the Romany word for gold, and *sauster*, so snottum may be yet another development from these words.

The earliest evidence in SLD's current research comes from Betsy Whyte's *Yellow on the Broom*, an autobiographical account of travellers' lives in the 1920s and '30s but written in 1979: '"Poor Charlie has had to go supperless to sleep tonight, but if I had had this with me," he said, as he pulled the heavy strong snottum out of the ground, "I would have killed all the redcoats that's in the glen."'

Duncan Williamson writing in 1994 his reminiscences of travelling life in *The Horsieman: Memories of a Traveller 1928–58* says: 'The tinsmith required a box of tin sheets, three feet by three feet; an anvil, made especially by a smith for making tin, which was portable... snottum or "pot stick" for hanging pots and kettles over the fire.'

So, although the written evidence comes from the late 20th century, the word was clearly used in earlier times. Again, as with many Scots words, much research is required.

Pauline Cairns Speitel

SOOK *verb* to suck

Many of the quotations for this word in the dictionary refer to suckling infants or young animals and this observation on animal husbandry comes from a 17th century manuscript by John Skene of Hallyards: 'Commonlie they lett not the calf sowcke longer than fowrtie dayis because if they sowck longer they become so browdden[1] that they cannot be halden of the paipe.'[2] Other assisduous sookers appear in a quotation in the *Thre Prestis of Pablis* (c.1500): 'The hungrie fleis wil cum and souk his blude.'

Some things in Scotland don't change. Attitudes to smoking, however, have hardened since *The Poetical Works of Alexander Craig of Rose-Craig* appeared in the early 17th century, when tobacco was very much a novelty: 'From pype of loame and for thy saike I souke, The flegm-attractiue far-fett Indian smouke.'

Sookin on a larger scale is described by Bellenden in his translation of Boece's *Chronicles of Scotland* (1531) as contributing to the tides: 'The see... sum times yettand out the tid, and sum times swelleand and soukand it in agane.' In *Essays of a Prentise in the Divine Art of Poesie* (1585), James VI muses on meteorology, 'When the sunne doth souk the vapours small Forth of the seas.'

Modern sookin gives rise to a number of disparaging expressions. The idea of sookin was extended somewhat ludicrously to unfledged birds to give similes for foolish or feeble persons. So a 'sookin teuchat'[3] lacks experience and John Galt in *The Howdie*[4] (1833) refers to a 'tottling creature, with no more sense than a sucking turkey'. Clinginess gets mocked by William Cross in *The Disruption* (1846): 'He depended on me owre lang, but I like nae sookin' stirks.'[5] Sookin in with the boss will not be appreciated by one's colleagues and any sycophant who does so will inevitably be labelled a sook.

Chris Robinson

---

[1] *intent*
[2] *holding the nipple*
[3] *lapwing*
[4] *midwife*
[5] *bullocks*

SOUTER *noun* a cobbler, a shoemaker

Souter appears in surnames from the early 13th century, which implies the trade is much older. Indeed, the Scots word is descended from Old English *suture* and we find *sutor* in Latin before that.

Soutering appears to have been a reserved occupation; *The Orygynale Cronykil of Scotland* by Andrew of Wyntoun (c.1420) records that, 'In Ingland than... wes left na man For... all war in Frawns¹ Bot sowteris, skynneris or marchawns.'² Alternatively, they may have been left behind for another reason. Adam Loutfut's 1494 manuscript claims 'Barbouris sowtaris writtaris & talyeouris... ar na worth for battell.' William Dunbar, however, appreciates their skills: 'Sowtaris, with schone³ weill maid and meit ye mend the faltis of illmaid feit', but even he has reservations: 'Latt nevir the soutteris have my skin, With uglie gumes to be gnawin.'

In his *Flyting*, Polwart used the insults 'creishie soutter, shoo clooter',⁴ and several quotations in the DSL associate souters with drunkenness or poverty. Stewart Robertson in *With Double Tongue* (1928) considers the unlikely day 'When bairns grow mensefu'⁵ a' at aince, and souters a' are sober'. Souter's brandy is another name for buttermilk and a souter's clod is a roll of coarse bread. Fergussons' *Proverbs* (c.1598) tell us the 'The sowters wife is worst shod.'

Nonetheless, souters seem content. Walter Gregor, in *Notes on the Folk-Lore of the North-East of Scotland* (1881), writes 'The following is called the "Souter's Grace": "What are we before thee, O King Crispin? Naething bit a parcel o' easy ozy sooter bodies, nae worth one old shoe to mend another. Yet thou hast given us leather to yark, and leather to bark, oot-seam awls, and in-seam awls, pincers and petrie-balls, lumps o' creesch and balls o' rosit, and batter in a cappie. Amen."'

Chris Robinson

---

¹ *France*
² *merchants*
³ *shoes*
⁴ *greasy shoemaker, shoe patcher*
⁵ *clever*

SPEEL *verb* to climb, clamber

The derivation of this word is obscure; the earliest recorded meaning in the DSL is: 'to perform as an acrobat' and dates from 1503. Later, it widens its meaning to include 'To mount, ascend to a height by climbing; to climb, clamber…' The OED suggests that it may originally derive from 'older Flemish or Low German *speler* (German: *spieler*) player, actor.'

At Christmas and other times when party invitations are forthcoming, speel comes to mind as a candidate for Word of the Week because of a reply in verse given by Robert Burns, writing in 1786, to just such an invitation: 'Sir, Yours this moment I unseal, And faith I'm gay and hearty! To tell the truth and shame the deil, I am as fou as Bartie: But Foorsday[1], sir, my promise leal[2], Expect me o' your partie, If on a beastie[3] I can speel, Or hurl[4] in a cartie. Yours, Robert Burns. Mauchline, Monday night, 10 o'clock.' The verse creates a clear mental picture of a slightly tipsy Burns trying to clamber onto his horse.

Most other examples in the DSL are centred round scaling less mobile objects than horses. In 1950, O Douglas in *Farewell to Priorsford* wrote: 'Naebody had ever tried to spiel thae rocks.' Figurative uses are well documented too. The following is from RW Thom's *Jock o Knowe*: 'Tam Gripper, then nae laird atweel, Maun[5] up the social ladder speel.' (Dumfries, 1877)

Pauline Cairns Speitel

---

[1] *Thursday*
[2] *loyal, faithfull*
[3] *horse*
[4] *ride in a wheeled vehicle*
[5] *must*

SPIRTLE *noun* porridge stick

You would not think that there could be much controversy about a simple kitchen implement but the humble spirtle, spurtil(l), spartle, spirl, spurl or spruttle, spell it how you will, has several varieties and uses.

My mother's spirtle, a simple wooden stick worn to a third of its original size with stirring of porridge and soup, was never put to such violent use as that recorded in *Papers submitted in Cases before the Court of Session: Cramond v. Allan* (1756), where we read: 'Her father would have her make the pottage for supper… She saw her father strike her mother at another time with the spurtle.' A spirtle is alternatively described in the DSL as a wooden or metal implement with a long handle and a flat blade used in baking for turning oatcakes, scones, etc and this is supported with quotations such as that from the *Transactions of the Dumfries and Galloway Natural History and Antiquarian Society* (1891): '"Yere cake's burnin…" "Make us a spurtle tae turn it wi', then."'

A theekin spirtle is flat-bladed instrument, sometimes forked, for pushing thatching straw into position on a roof and, in the production of linen, a spirtle is a flat stick or bat for beating flax. A spirtle-grup or spirtle-shot is a sharp pain in the side and the DSL provides a remarkable folk remedy culled from *Manuscript Notes on North East Scotland Folk-Lore*, in the library of The Folk-Lore Society, London, given by JE Crombie, (c.1890): 'A child should receive the kidneys of a hare the first kind of flesh to eat. This prevents the child from taking "the spurtle shot", the sharp pain that strikes one in the side when running or walking fast.' If you manage to try it out, please let us know if it works.

Chris Robinson

STAIRHEID RAMMY *noun* a quarrel between neighbours

A stairheid rammy was, indeed, originally a quarrel between neighbours dwelling in Scotland's tenements and the earliest example we have in the DSL comes from *The Herald* of 5 November 1994: 'Stairheid rammies have continued into the third and fourth generations, and the only possible "extirpation", namely banishment, has been removed so all that is left is to deal with each incident as it arises.'

Quarrels between neighbours seem to have been a feature of Scottish tenement life and stairheid rows have been recorded as early as 1928 as this example from the *Dundee Evening Telegraph* of 26 September of that year shows: 'A "stairheid" row at 58 North William Street, was recounted at Dundee Police Court this morning.'

Language, however, is fluid and always shifting meanings so the stairheid rammy has taken on a figurative slant as this example from the *Daily Record* of 10 February 2017 shows: 'A late night stairheid rammy in the Commons on Monday as the SNP complained bitterly about being talked out of the Brexit debate.' And this figurative element also passes into the world of football as Aidan Smith writing in *The Scotsman* of 14 August 2016 tells us: 'A fair old stairheid rammy, then, and Walker can count on more choruses of disapproval at away grounds when his ban is over, but how can such incidents be cut out the game?'

So, the original use of the term seems to have been taken over by a description of any quarrel between footballing or political opponents.

Pauline Cairns Speitel

STOOKIE *noun* gypsum, a plaster cast, an effigy

This word is being topically typed with one hand. It comes from Italian *stucco* but originates in Old High German *stukki* (a fragment). Like stucco in English, it means fine plaster, but its orthopedic application is purely Scots. The shared sense is demonstrated in the *Proceedings of the Scottish Anthropological & Folklore Society* (1948): 'When the doorstep had been washed, the careful housewife would draw designs and patterns with white "stookie".' An exchange in Alan Spence's *Way to Go* (1998) illustrates the Scots usage: '"You want to be buried in a plaster cast?" I asked him. "Like a mummy?" He shook his head, laughed. "Naw! I want a box, but just a simple white job. And I want everybody to write on it, wee messages and that, drawings." "Like a stookie. Right." "I always mind it when I broke my arm. The things people wrote on it!"'

A stookie mannie or mumie is a plaster statue. We have an interesting variant spelling from Banffshire in 1930: 'The wife bocht a stooga mannie this foreneen fae a foreign-lookin bodie.' 'Like a stookie' means immobile, unresponsive and stupified, like this character in JL Waugh's *Cute McCheyne* (1917): 'I juist stood like a stookie, thowless an' donnert.'[1] This next gem comes from *The Scotsman* (2002): 'So it came as no surprise when he described the Scottish Office minister Allan Stewart as a "stookie" at Scottish Questions. What did come as a surprise yesterday, though, was when the bods at Hansard sent him a memo, asking: "What is a stookie? How is it spelt? Was it used in reference to undersecretary of State?"' Since we can only assume the House of Commons library has a copy of the the *Concise Scots Dictionary*, which defines the word as 'foolish person; blockhead', we can only conclude that the compilers of Hansard are the biggest stookies of them all.

Chris Robinson

---

[1] *lethargic and dazed*

STRAMASH *noun* uproar, commotion

My personal definition of stramash is a happy chaos but, like most words, it can mean different things to different people. The DSL defines it as an uproar or commotion and these can lead to trouble. So a stramash can also be a squabble, accident or disaster. The dictionary quotations show there is little new under the sun. We have stramashes in finance. A quotation dating from 1803 in the *Three Banks Review* (1959) relates: 'A very unexpected stramash occurred in our Accomptant's office two days ago.' They can unsettle governments, as threatened in John Galt's *The Ayrshire Legatees* (1821): 'She will raise sic a stramash, that she will send the whole government into the air.' In similar vein, John Buchan in *Witch Wood* (1927) writes 'The folk of Woodilee are ready enough for any stramash in kirk or state.'

Stramash also appears as a verb meaning to be rowdy, and we have yet another meaning JFS Gordon's *The Book of the Chronicles of Keith, Grange, Ruthven, Cairnie and Botriphne*: 'Choking the lums with a divot which occasionally stramashed the Tea Pots.'

It is first recorded in Yorkshire as a verb meaning smash to pieces, as in that last quotation. Therefore, the *New English Dictionary* hypothesises it may be an altered intensive form of smash and argues against the Scottish lexicographer John Jamieson's ingenious suggestion of connection with Italian *strammazone* (a downward slash with a rapier in fencing). The DSL adjudicates, 'There is nothing inherently impossible in the adoption of a fencing term... but the phonology, esp. the accentuation, is difficult to explain and earlier historical evidence for development of meaning is lacking. The word may in fact be a corruption of O.Fr. (Old French) escarmoche or one of its many forms... which have produced English scrimmage, skirmish.' Etymology is certainly not an exact science.

Chris Robinson

STRAVAIG *verb* to roam about without purpose; *noun* a stroll

There are various definitions of stravaig in the DSL but for this article I will concentrate on the above two. The DSL's first definition is written in the language of the day: 'To roam, wander idly, gad about in an aimless casual manner' and the first example is an Edinburgh one from the 1773 edition of Robert Fergusson's *Poems*: 'Pith, that helps them to stravaig Our ilka cleugh and ilka craig.' The example is closely followed by one from his great admirer Robert Burns from a letter of 1787: 'Some notion o my land-lowperlike[1] stravaugin.' Note Rab's spelling which probably reflects how he would have pronounced it.

Folk still go stravaigin in modern times: 'I will never forget Tuesday evening in particular, having spent an afternoon stravaiging among the nooks and crannies of Stromness...' (*The Herald*, 9 June 1993) And from the 21st century, we have the following from *The Scotsman* of 7 March 2018: 'It's just over 15 years since the passing into law of the Land Reform (Scotland) Act – the wonderful piece of legislation which, among other things, gives us all the right to stravaig freely around the countryside – regardless of who owns it – as long as we behave ourselves...' When we Scots have a wee wander we still call it a stravaig as in the oral example from 2004: 'We went for a wee stravaig roond Arthur's Seat.'

Outlander gets everywhere these days and the following example illustrates how stravaig is used to mean a visit: 'The penultimate day takes in a visit to the infamous battle site at Culloden – site of the last pitched battle to be fought on British soil – before touring the Wardlaw Mausoleum and Clava Cairns. Day four features a stravaig to three more Outlander locations at Tulloch Ghru, Loch an Eilean and Ord Ban.'

The word is probably a form of an Older Scots word *extravage*.

Pauline Cairns Speitel

---

[1] *leaping, bounding*

STUSHIE *noun* a fuss

If you look up stushie as a 'headword' in the online DSL, all you will find is the starling, otherwise known as a stuckie. Although a flock of starlings might make a right stushie, this is not the word we want. A 'full entry' search, however, takes us where we want to go. This is a useful tip for users of the online dictionary. It gets around the problem of spelling variations. Under stashie (also stashy, stachie; stushie, stushy; steeshie, steishie, stishie), we find it means 'an uproar, commotion or brawl'. It is often slipped into Scottish English, but most Scots are aware that stushie is not an English word. Nevertheless, it is widely used and has even been heard on Radio 4's Today programme from the lips of James Nauchtie. It is the ideal word to cover all levels of political, religious or domestic fuss, internationally or locally.

Minimal stushie is implied on James Stewart's *Sketches of Scottish Character* (1857): 'The weel-timed whisper'd wheesht aye lays The sma'est stushy that they raise.' When some scandal becomes the 'speak o the place' you might, like Grace Webster in *Ingliston* (1840) say 'The hail toun's been in a stushie about it.' On a truly global level, we have Hugh MacDiarmid's line from 'Somersault', published in *Pennywheep* (1926): 'I lo'e the stishie o' Earth in space.'

Stushies can become violent. Douglas Lipton implies anticipatory delight in *The Day I Met the Queen Mother* (1990): 'Whit a stooshie! – Ah'll haud yir jaikits.' Some even get out of hand as in R Sim's *Legends of Strathisla* (1862) where intervention becomes necessary and 'The Earl o' Huntly was aye ane o' the true hearts that was sent for to red[1] the stachie.' That was one stushie 'the weel-timed whisper'd wheesht' could not quell.

Chris Robinson

---

[1] *intervene, separate*

SUMPH *noun* a simpleton, a foolish person

'A Sumph... is a chiel to whom Natur has denied ony considerable share o' understaunin', without hae'n chose to mak him just altogether an indisputable idiot.' This 1831 quotation, cited in the OED from J Wilson's *Noctes Ambrosianae lix*, in *Blackwood's Edinburgh Magazine*, provides a good indication of what a sumph is.

However, seeing how the word is used in practice can be more informative than trying to provide a neat definition. The following quotations from the DSL tell us a bit more about the nature of sumphs.

In Archibald McIlroy's *When Lint was in the Bell* (1897), someone is described as 'Naethin' but a great muckle sumph – a bigger fael[1] than a' even tuk ye for', and in Fred Urquhart's *Time Will Knit* (1938): '...She was just takin' a rise oot o' him, but the muckle sumph thought she was in earnest.' More recently, in Liz Lochhead's *Tartuffe* (1985), a character asks: 'How could it come up Orgon's humph To abandon his dochter tae yon big sumph?' These examples describe sumphs as 'great muckle' and 'big' and size certainly seems to be part of sumphness. You wouldn't call a skinny wee person a sumph.

Although usually male, there is the occasional reference to a female sumph, as in this 1933 quotation from the *Scots Magazine*: 'She'd grown a great sumph of a woman.' Interestingly, this also implies largeness.

However, there isn't always a reference to size, and the general impression is that a sumph is gormless or spineless rather than merely stupid. For example, in Robin Jenkins' *The Thistle and the Grail* (1994) someone says: 'you're such a sumph that if you did take the job as barman you'd develop into a drunkard. Your politeness would be the ruin of you.'

Ann Ferguson

---

[1] *fool*

SWALLIE *noun* an alcoholic drink

During the festive season, many of us will indulge in a 'wee swallie'.

Swallie as a noun was first noted by the editors of the 2005 supplement to the DSL in Michael Munro's *The Original Patter* (1985): '**swally** Pronounced to rhyme with rally, this is a local version of swallow: "She's swallied the hail lot!" A swally can be a drink or a drinking session: "Fancy a wee swally?"' Note that he indicates the original meaning first.

Later, in the 1990s, Ian Pattison's Rab C Nesbit informs us that while minding his own business: 'I wiz jist havin a wee swallie...'

In earlier times, many Scottish households did not routinely keep alcohol at home except at new year. This was noted as late as 29 December 1994 in the *Daily Record*, illustrating how important the selection of the New Year bottle still was: 'Like marriage and cinemas, the purchase of the Ne'erday swally is something that cannot be entered into lightly.'

A swallie can mean anything from a 'wee refreshment' to a longer drinking session. We have a plural example during another festive period from *The List* of 3–17 December 1998: 'Flush with success and a few celebratory swallies, the bright lights of the casino beckoned us in and sucked us dry.' This would seem to encourage us not to drink and gamble.

Swallie is still in current use in the 21st century and still during the festive period with a beer designed to slake the thirst of Santa after his toils as in this example from *The Herald* of 12 December 2013: 'Beer lovers can savour Santa's Swallie from Perth's Inveralmond Brewery.'

Pauline Cairns Speitel

SYBOE *noun* spring onion

Hou weel dae ye ken yer Spring ingans? Syboes add flavour to the DSL in a surprisingly large number of literal and figurative quotations. As regards their monetary value, in 1552, The *Dundee Burgh Court Records* itemises the purchase of 'xv dussane of beddis of sybowis for xij s. the dussane'. They were highly valued by consumers as the *Journals of Sir John Lauder* (1665–7) show: 'Some likes[1] some sibows, beets or such like things and this is their delicates.' In June 1997, *The Sunday Times* made mouths water with the description of 'a really good roast quail, for example, which had been marinaded in sesame oil and soy sauce then roasted before receiving a garnish of intensely grilled syboes'.

Less happily, *Glasgow Burgh Records* (1575) describes a woman's misfortune, which resulted 'In castyng of hir doune… and skailing[2] of hir sybois' and *Northern Notes and Queries* (1889) records that in 1653 'pulling sybous on the Lord's day' was a matter for reproach.

In figurative use, there seems to have been frequent comparison between biting the end off a syboe and beheading: 'I have beheaded your duke like a sybow' (1675) exemplifies this gruesome simile in W Crammond's *The Castle and the Lords of Balveny*. The crispness of the onion stem is apparent in 'This day the head is as clean taken off the house of Cowthally, as you cowld strike off the head of a sybba', as James Somerville wrote in the *Memorie of the Somervilles* (1679).

Overall, syboes have very positive connotations. AS Robertson, in *The Provost of Glendookie* (1894), tells us 'If mair sybies were eaten there would be fewer doctors' and Syboe is even used affectionately as a nickname for an inhabitant of Girvan in Ayrshire where growing spring onions was a speciality.

Chris Robinson

---

[1] *leeks*
[2] *spilling, upturning*

TENT *noun* attention, care, heed, notice

The above meaning of tent first appears in the DSL in an example from John Barbour's Bruce (1375): 'To the rerward[1] na tent tuk he.'

In modern Scots, we are more likely to encounter tent in the phrase to 'tak tent' meaning to pay attention or, more specifically, to beware as in the following from a poem collected by Francis Child: 'He gently tirled the pin;[2] The lassie taking tent unto the door she went.' (*Grey Cock*, 1769) In Sir Walter Scott's *Old Mortality*, he gives a warning about a spirited horse: 'Take tent o' yourself, for my horse is not very chancy.' The poet Violet Jacob in her 1918 collection *More Songs* warns someone to be on their guard and to 'Tak' tent o' an Angus lad like me'.

In that late 20th century, our former Makar Liz Lochhead issued a warning to the then main political leaders which still has an eerie resonance today: 'So – watch out Margaret Thatcher, and tak' tent Neil Kinnock, Or we'll tak' the United Kingdom and brekk it like a bannock.' (*Bagpipe Muzak*, 1991)

Even in the 21st century it's still a popular phrase here denoting incredulity at the swift passage of time: 'Michty its hard tae tak tent o e fac aat here we are heidin wir wye tae the eyn o September already…' this observation comes from the *Inverurie Herald* of 28 September 2015.

And finally, a warning to the new president elect from the *The Press and Journal* of 12 November 2016 quoting an old Ballad: 'Fit an image tae portray tae the warl an baith shid tak tent o that sang as it tells it aa wi "folks fa and never rise again wha never fell before; There's aye a muckle slippery steen at ilka body's[3] door".'

Pauline Cairns Speitel

---

[1] *the rear guard of an army*

[2] *a tirling pin was a kind of door knocker*

[3] *everybody's*

THRAPPLE *noun* throat, windpipe, gullet

The first recorded example comes from Barbour's Bruce (1375): 'He... hyt the formast in the hals Till throppill and vassand yeid in twa.'[1] Several quotations in the DSL are violent, including Sir Walter Scott's in *Rob Roy* (1817): '"When we had a Scotch Parliament, Pate," says I (and deil rax their thrapples that reft us o't!).'[2] Worse, the *Letters of John Ramsay of Ochtertyre*, (1801) describe 'One of the chief's ancestors who said the sweetest morsel he ever ate was the thrapple of an Englishman.'

Almost two centuries after it is found in Scots, thrapple or thropple makes an appearance in English, chiefly in the sense of a horse's neck. It never achieved the currency south of the border that it has here. The phrase 'to weet yer thrapple' is still in common use, as it was in Robert Fergusson's time (1773): 'The dinner done, for brandy strang They cry, to weet their thrapple.' John R Allan in *North-East Lowlands of Scotland* (1952) prefers a local beverage. 'Whisky', he tells us, 'should be matured in a cask for at least five or seven years to lose any harshness and bite; for it is not worthy to be drunk till it goes over the thrapple like milk and then glows up like a rising sun. If Yer thrapple shuts ticht wi' the kink-hoast'[3] (*The Press and Journal*, 30 January 1970), you can only dream of the satisfaction of 'Hoasting up a thrapple-redding cough' as described in the *Poems* of John Walker (1882). Staying with hoarseness of the thrapple, the expression 'a dry thrapple' was used by sailors as a name for the curlew, which, like many other creatures, could not be named at sea without inviting bad luck.

Chris Robinson

---

[1] *he hit the foremost in the neck so that gullet and windpipe went in two*

[2] *and devil twist their thrapples that bereft us of it.*

[3] *whooping cough*

TUMSHIE *noun* a turnip

Tumshie is a word of obscure origin. The DSL suggests that is could be a children's version of 'turmet', a Scots form of English turnip.

It seems to be a relatively late additon to DSL with the first example dating from 1947: 'Gee we hid a lot o' fun pinchin' totties[1] an' tumshies.' (JF Hendry *Fernie Brae*).

However, Santa is not the only one with access to elves at this time of year and here at SLD, our elves have discovered an earlier example from *The Falkirk Herald* of 18 August 1923: 'Stolen fruit is always sweetest they say, and perhaps the same remark applied to the stolen "tumshie".' Obviously, tumshies seem to have been the target of opportunistic thieves.

Although, ten years later, this example follows again from *The Falkirk Herald*, where the tumshie is part of a special meal: 'Supper consisting of "tatties and baked tumshies and potted heid", was afterwards partaken of.' (28 January 1933)

Of course, before the advent of the pumpkin, the tumshie lantern or tumshie leerie was an essential part of a guiser's Halloween equipment as illustrated here from the *Kirkintilloch Advertiser* of 3 November 1943: 'There were no "tumshie leeries" to be seen this Hallowe'en.' No fun for guisers during wartime, then.

From West Lothian in 1973, we are also told that a tumshie gowk is another name for a scarecrow from the habit of using a tumshie for the head.

Scots being Scots did manage to turn this round into a term of abuse for a stupid person: 'Brainy folk will thank him while tumshies won't have a clue.' (*The Sunday Herald*, 8 April 2007)

Pauline Cairns Speitel

---

[1] *potatoes*

VAUNTIE *adjective* proud, vain, boastful

We Scots are often reluctant to blow our own trumpet, fearing a put-down from someone who 'kent yer faither'. Many of our words for proud are quite reductive and imply that someone has got a bit above themselves, like bigsie, or windy, or pauchtie. Vauntie can be used that way but it can also have positive connotations and so it appears in William Jamie's *Muse of the Mearns* (1844): 'Indeed, Gudewife, ye're dear to me, Of you I am right vaunty.' James Lumsden in *Sheep-Head and Trotters* (1892) uses it in the sense of pleased rather than vain: 'We've got a judge and referee (Cried I, right vauntie!).' This also seems the intended emotion in Robert Muir's *Mystery of Muncraig* (1900): 'A window that my neighbour the grocer was very vaunty about.'

In Burns' *Tam o' Shanter* (1790), the young witch is not being criticised for her pride in her sark: 'In longitude tho' sorely scanty, It was her best, she was vauntie.' Occasionally it is used of the clothes themselves, rather than the wearer. In this case, the garments may be ostentatious or just jaunty or smart. So this description in *Modern Scottish Poets* (1860) is intended to be complimentary: 'Wi' bonnet sae vaunty, an' owerlay¹ sae clean.'

Vauntie is a word that has come up in the world and risen above the more pejorative flavour of its origins. With the addition of its adjective-forming suffix, it comes from the noun 'vaunt', which, in Older Scots, denotes all the sinfulness of pride. In Adam Abell's *The Roit or Quheill of Tyme* (c.1538), we find it paired with vainglory, and William Dunbar (c.1508) censures 'Sic vant of wostouris with hairtis in sinfull staturis'.² By contrast, vauntie is a useful word for someone who might have a guid conceit o thirsel but stops well short of the deadly sin.

Chris Robinson

---

¹ *necktie, cravat*
² *Such pride of boasters with hearts in sinful states.*

WEAN *noun* child

We have sometimes featured words now associated with the North East, although they once had a much wider currency. This week, we look at a word which many people associate with Glasgow. Glasgow authors have used it to great effect, as in this poignant quotation from John and Willy Maley's *From The Calton To Catalonia* (1990): 'Picture it. The Calton. Fair Fortnight. 1937. Full of Eastern promise. Wimmen windae hingin. Weans greetin for pokey hats.¹ Grown men, well intae their hungry thirties, slouchin at coarners, skint as a bairn's knees.'

However, wean, a running together of wee and ane, first appears in the dictionaries with Leadhills-born poet Allan Ramsay's *The Gentle Shepherd* (1725): 'Troth, my Niece is a right dainty we'an.' This is followed by an Aberdeenshire quotation in *Helenore* (1768) by Alexander Ross: 'The dentyest wean bony Jane fuish² hame.' Weans, not always dainty, appear in Burns, Scott, Hogg and Stevenson.

Weans may mean offspring generally, be they laddie weans or lassie weans, but Anna Blair in *The Rowan on the Ridge* (1980) is more precise, placing weanhood between infancy and adolescence: '...a wean and a baby whose names he had not caught, and the dour halflin' Bryce, who had looked him up and down and seemed as if he might have checked his teeth or hooves before taking him on to labour.'

Even bairnish adults can be called weanly. PH Waddell's 1871 version of *Psalm 119* gives 'Fu' clear comes a blink o' yer words, makin wyss the weanliest chiel' and, in figurative usage, we clearly imagine the flying leather described in James Denniston's *The Battle of Craignilder* (1832): 'But sword or axe gied weanly whacks Compared wi' Geordy's flail, man.' So, although wean is common in west-central Scotland, it is by no means restricted to that area.

Chris Robinson

---

¹ *ice-cream cones*
² *fetched*

WERSH *adjective* insipid, feeble

The first example of wersh in the DSL is from Henryson's *The Tale of Orpheus and Erudices his Quene* (a1500): 'Erudices... Rycht warsch and wan and walowit[1] as the wede', where it meant sickly-looking.

Later, it was often used for food or drink, meaning insipid or tasteless, as in this from Stewart A Robertson's *With Double Tongue* (1928): 'But water's wersh when ye're drouthy for yill.'[2] More specifically, it meant lacking in salt, as in the *Hawick News* (1972): 'Next to the dislike for lumpy porridge was that of wairsh porridge.'

Extending the meaning beyond food, it is stated in WL Watson's *Sir Sergeant* (1899) that: 'A half-done deed and a half-boiled egg are wersh things', and in Sir Walter Scott's *Old Mortality* (1816): 'The Worcester man was but wersh parritch, neither gude to fry, boil, nor sup cauld.'

Wersh was also used to refer to a variety of things that could be insipid, dull or otherwise lacking sparkle. Of language, it meant tame and uninspiring, as in this from RM Fergusson's *A Village Poet* (1897): 'The jokes which tickle the palates o' the Southerners are gey wersh.' Referring to music, it meant flat or thin, as in 'Their tone though sweetish, is wersh, like the tone o' the floot' from John Wilson's *Noctes Ambrosianae* (in *Blackwood's Magazine*, 1826).

In more modern usage, wersh is also used to mean sour or bitter, as in Hugh MacDiarmid's *Sangschaw* (1925): 'Wersh is the vinegar. And the sword is sharp.' Applied to weather, it means raw, cold or damp: in SR Crockett's *The Raiders* (1894) we read that 'The yellow mist had a wersh unkindly feel about it.'

However, in the opinion of the *The Glasgow Herald* in 1948, 'Wersh as a synonym for bitter is a turgid usage.'

Ann Ferguson

---

[1] *withered, faded*
[2] *ale*

WIDDERSHINS *adverb* in the wrong direction

This comes from Middle Low German *weddersinnes* or Middle Dutch *wedersins*. In the early quotations we have, it frequently refers to hair standing widdershins in response to some alarming experience 'that will gar all their hearts tremble and their haire start widdershin' (David Calderwood's *History of the Kirk of Scotland* 1570).

In other contexts, there is no doubt what the wrong direction usually is. *The Scotsman* (1989) gives us a clue, pointing out an error made by a well-known weather presenter: 'He at least should know that wind round anti-cyclones goes widdershins.' Going counterclockwise or against the motion of the sun is not only wrong but inauspicious. Sir Walter Scott in the *Fair Maid of Perth* (1828) describes: 'A very ancient custom which consists in going three times round the body of a dead or living person, imploring blessing upon him. The Deasil[1] must be performed sun-ways... If misfortune is imprecated, the party moves withershins.'

We find a lot of evidence in accounts of witchcraft, such as this 1697 quotation from *A History of the Witches of Renfrewshire*: 'Upon the pronouncing of some words, and turning himself about wider-shins, that is turning himself round from the right hand to the left, contrary to the natural course of the sun.' *The Records of Elgin* (1545) give us this glimpse of a scantily clad witch: '...the said Margarat Baffour vas ane huyr and ane wyche and that sche ʒeid widersonnis about mennis hous sark alane.'[2] The *New Statistical Account* (1845) records that Shetland fishermen 'when about to proceed to the fishing, think they would have bad luck, if they were to row the boat "withershins" about.' However, on a romantic note, the poet Allan Ransay declares (1724): 'The starns[3] shall gang withershins ere I deceive thee.'

Chris Robinson

---

[1] *a clockwise walk round a person to bring good fortune*
[2] *They said Margarat Baffour was a whore and a witch and she went widdershins around men's houses wearing only a chemise.*
[3] *stars*

YEUKIE *adjective* itchy

As the midgies and clegs get into full biting mode, this is a useful word to have on the tip of your tongue. As WD Cocker explained, with the voice of experience, in *Further Poems* (1935): 'Yae cleg-bite's bad, but twa's unlucky, The mair ye scart the mair it's yeuckie.'

There are other causes of yeukiness, however. It is well known and documented in *Scottish Notes and Queries* (1891), that 'A "yeuky loof" or itching palm is regarded as indicative of coming favours.' Other causes are found in the *Forfar Dispatch* (1947): 'I wiz juist giein my lum a bit sweepie, fin I gies a sneeze – the shuit garred my nose turn uikie', and in William P Milne's *Eppie Elrick* (1955): 'Sair bitties is aye yokie fin' ey're hellin.'[1]

Scrapie, the affliction of sheep, is also known as euky pine, and a yokie knot is a heat spot. Kittlie feet can be brought on by a toetapping tune such as the one played by the wee herd in Charles Murray's *The Whistle* (1909): 'The feet o' ilka man an' beast gat youkie when he played.'

A tickle in the throat features in Saxon's (R de B Trotter's) *Galloway Gossip Sixty Years Ago* (1879): 'Davie was awfu yeuky about the thrapple, and naething wad help it but whiskey.' Relief, according to the DSL, may be obtained in a number of ways. The poet Ramsay (1719) gives us: 'We like Nags whase Necks are yucky, Ha'e us'd our Teeth.' David Davidson indelicately writes in *Thoughts on the Seasons* (1889) 'Unto thy smooth'ning tongue they fairly turn Their yeuky rumps.'

For some itches, such as love, however, there is no remedy as recounted by James Cromar in *The Prodigal's Wife* (1892): 'I hed a yokiness aboot the hert that I couldna get in to claw.'

Chris Robinson

---

[1] *Sore bits are always yeukie when they're healing.*

YULE *noun* Christmas

Whether you celebrate Yule on 25 December or Auld Yule on 5 January, you may be thinking about your Christmas dinner. Allan Ramsay (1717) had high expectations of 'A bra' Goose Pye'. According to one of William Taylor's Poems (1787), he too celebrated in style 'About Yule-time an' Hogmenai, Some chuckies an' a yowe we fell.'[1] Others less fortunate took delight in simpler treats. *Blackwood's Magazine* (1821) describes 'The prevailing Christmas dish among the common people and peasantry... the national one of fat brose, otherwise denominated Yule brose... after breakfast, or at dinner, the brose was made, generally in a large punch-bowl, the mistress of the ceremonies dropping in a gold ring among the oatmeal. The person who was so fortunate as to get the ring in their spoon, was to be the first married.'

Scottish Notes and Queries (1925) tells us: 'The baking of Yeel bannocks was another auspicious event. These bannocks were composed of beaten eggs, oatmeal and milk, and were baked on the girdle. Prior to the baking the fortune of each unmarried person present was read by some one skilled in such lore. Each chose an egg and gave it to the fortune-teller.'

In the North-East, the Yeel couple or the Yeel fish, usually a smoked haddock, was served to each member of the family as a special Christmas treat all to be washed down with Yule ale, recalled by William Watson in *Glimpses o Auld Lang Syne* (1903): 'The earliest recollections I have of Christmas are associated... with my being dispatched to Burnie's "chop" for hops, ginger and a big flagon for treacle, with which ingredients and malt from the "Canal Heid", my mother brewed the Yule ale.'

Chris Robinson

---

[1] *At Yule time and Hogmanay, some chickens and ewes we kill*

Luath Press Limited

committed to publishing well written books worth reading

LUATH PRESS takes its name from Robert Burns, whose little collie Luath (*Gael.*, swift or nimble) tripped up Jean Armour at a wedding and gave him the chance to speak to the woman who was to be his wife and the abiding love of his life. Burns called one of the 'Twa Dogs' Luath after Cuchullin's hunting dog in Ossian's *Fingal*.

Luath Press was established in 1981 in the heart of Burns country, and is now based a few steps up the road from Burns' first lodgings on Edinburgh's Royal Mile. Luath offers you distinctive writing with a hint of unexpected pleasures.

Most bookshops in the UK, the US, Canada, Australia, New Zealand and parts of Europe, either carry our books in stock or can order them for you. To order direct from us, please send a £sterling cheque, postal order, international money order or your credit card details (number, address of cardholder and expiry date) to us at the address below. Please add post and packing as follows: UK – £1.00 per delivery address; overseas surface mail – £2.50 per delivery address; overseas airmail – £3.50 for the first book to each delivery address, plus £1.00 for each additional book by airmail to the same address. If your order is a gift, we will happily enclose your card or message at no extra charge.

Luath Press Limited
543/2 Castlehill
The Royal Mile
Edinburgh EH1 2ND
Scotland
Telephone: +44 (0)131 225 4326 (24 hours)
email: sales@luath. co.uk
Website: www. luath.co.uk